SEW wiLD

Creating with STiTCh and miXED MeDiA

ALiSa BuRKE

INTERWEAVE.
interweave.com

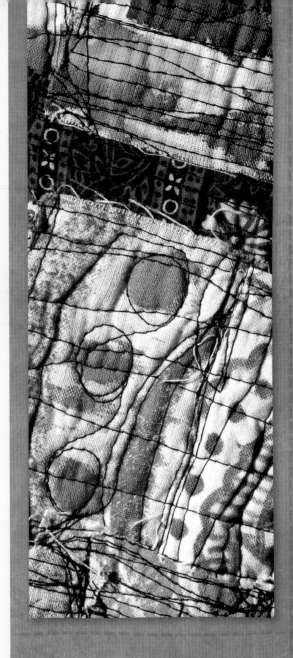

Interweave Press LLC
201 East Fourth Street
Loveland, CO 80637
interweave.com

Printed in China by Asia Pacific Offset Ltd.

Library of Congress
Cataloging-in-Publication Data

Burke, Alisa.
Sew wild : creating with stitch and mixed-
media / Alisa Burke.
    p. cm.
 Includes bibliographical references and
index.
 ISBN 978-1-59668-350-1
1. Textile crafts. I. Title.
TT699.B87 2011
646.2'044--dc22

2011002105

10 9 8 7 6 5 4 3 2 1

EDITOR   Elaine Lipson
ART DIRECTOR   Liz Quan
DESIGNER   Lee Calderon
ILLUSTRATOR   Ann Sabin Swanson
PRODUCTION   Katherine Jackson
PHOTOGRAPHY   Joe Coca
PHOTO STYLIST   Ann Sabin Swanson
HAIR AND MAKEUP   Jessica Shinyeda
DVD CONTENT PRODUCER Rebecca Campbell
VIDEOGRAPHER   Garrett Evans

Dedication

This book is dedicated to my mom, who taught me that anything can be made by hand, who had the patience to teach me how to sew, who took me to craft supply stores at an early age, who showed me how to use a glue gun, and who taught me how to clean spilled paint off the rug. Thank you for always encouraging me to draw, paint, and create, thank you for supporting my crazy ideas even when they didn't make sense, and for helping me think of more crazy ideas. Thank you for being such a powerful example of a strong and creative woman. You are my muse.

Acknowledgments

A huge thank you to my editor, Elaine Lipson, for the support, attention to detail, understanding, and most of all, for taking my words and transforming them into something wonderful. Thank you to Rebecca Campbell, Lee Calderon, Liz Quan, Joe Coca, and the entire Interweave team—I am forever grateful that all of you believed in my wild and crazy ideas and helped to make them real.

Thank you to my husband, Andy, who gives me time to myself, space to create, freedom to make a mess, and the encouragement to follow my dreams. Thank you to my family, who continue to love, support, and inspire me each and every day. All of you rock my world!

Contents

BONUS DVD

Putting It All Together: Techniques Demo

Bonus Project: Fabric Flags

Bonus Demo: Fabric Flowers

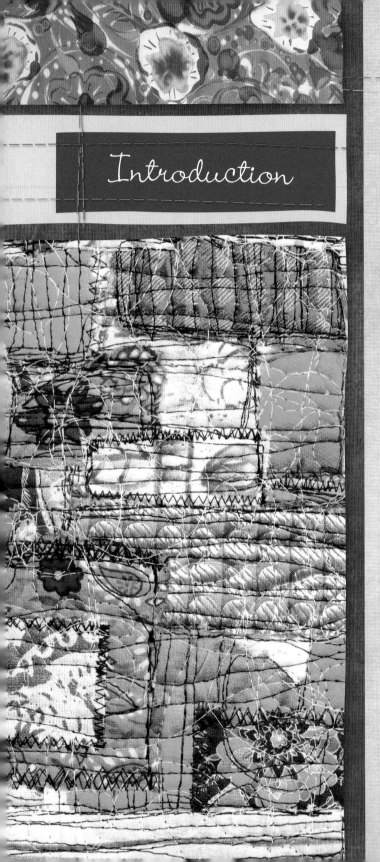

Introduction

I WAS EIGHT YEARS OLD when my mom taught me how to sew. I remember sitting next to her at the table as she showed me how to thread the needle and insert the bobbin. I listened to her explanations of how to follow a pattern; I remember stretching my short legs under the table to the pedal, apprehensively pushing down, slowly guiding fabric through the machine as she looked on and gently encouraged me.

I also remember getting frustrated, crying, losing my temper, struggling with focus, and straining to understand patterns. While I have fond memories of the time spent bonding with my mom, I don't have fond memories of the process—because back then I hated sewing. Measurements gave me anxiety, patterns made no sense, following directions left me frustrated, and I just didn't seem to have the patience that was required to follow the steps and finish a project.

After a few years of trying, of failed projects, of more frustration and annoyance, I gave up and ditched sewing. I went on to pursue art, which was my true passion. I took drawing lessons, spent hours in art classes, and studied fine art in college. I fell in love with being an artist, with learning all that I could. I studied different mediums and developed my own style. I was painting, drawing, printmaking, carving, molding, and getting my hands in anything and everything that was creative. I discovered my creative process.

FROM FRUSTRATION TO FREEDOM

And then one day (insert twenty years) I rediscovered sewing—but this time it was on my terms. After all those art classes, discipline, and time spent understanding my learning style and developing my creative voice, I suddenly had the desire and the mindset to try to sew again. I bought a cheap sewing machine and spent the first few weeks getting reacquainted with my old nemesis. Instead of giving in to frustration, I decided to treat the process as I treated all of my other creative learning. I let myself play and have fun, I gave myself permission to fail, I broke rules, I lost myself in experimentation.

By the end of those few weeks, I was smitten with sewing and couldn't quite remember why I ever gave up on it. Before I knew it, I had developed my own sewing style that was rooted in making art. It wasn't about following steps or patterns—it was about being messy, expressive, and wild. I began stitching on painted canvas, creating my own fabrics, and designing all kinds of funky projects and accessories.

These days, my sewing machine is just as important as my pens, brushes, and paint. It's a tool that has completely changed my concept of art, and I continue to find new and creative ways to integrate sewing with alternative materials and projects. I use my sewing machine to draw, make marks, create texture, journal, and build compositions. I use it to make accessories and assemble art, to attach things, create layers, establish color, and so much more. I now see that those early years of failed sewing projects and frustration were necessary in my journey. They paved the way for me to discover how great it feels to break free and go wild.

HOW TO USE THIS BOOK

This book is all about my style, my process, and my messy and wild approach to sewing. Whether you are a beginner or a seasoned pro, my goal is to inspire you to look at fabric, alternative materials, and sewing in a different way. I want to break down the stigma that often goes along with sewing—that it's scary, that there are rules to follow, that you have to be technical and always use a pattern. Instead I want to encourage you to experiment, find your style, embrace mistakes, be messy, let loose, and explore.

This book has a variety of techniques and ideas that can be used alone or mixed together. You won't find lots of technical or traditional information in *Sew Wild*, but you will find simple concepts and techniques that have inspired me to break free with my own sewing. I'll introduce you to my favorite tools and materials, along with information on using color and pattern and finding inspiration. Then I'll share techniques for creating your own fabric and altering materials, together with the basics of wild stitching. Finally, I'll bring all of the techniques and concepts together in a group of simple sewing projects. My hope is that *Sew Wild* will provide an inspiring foundation for ideas that can be altered to fit your own imagination.

MATERIALS AND toOLs

I AM A FIRM BELIEVER IN SIMPLE SUPPLIES. In my creative life I don't have time to search for specialty products; I don't have the money to purchase lots of supplies; and to be honest, my studio is already overflowing with perfectly usable things. Most of the techniques and projects in this book make use of very basic supplies and the techniques allow for plenty of flexibility, so you can put your own twist on them. To get started creating, make sure you have enough supplies on hand—you never know when creativity will strike!

Surface Design Tools

When I'm creating, I always make sure that I have plenty of tools that I'm comfortable using. Often I splurge on one or two favorite items—maybe a special brush or set of fabric markers—and then challenge myself to be creative and simple with everything else that I have.

MARKERS AND PENS

Pens and markers are very versatile tools for decorating fabric. I use both permanent markers, such as Sharpies, and pens and markers designed for use on fabric. Most markers come in a variety of colors, and while my color preference is typically black, I always recommend keeping a variety of favorite colors on hand. Markers also come in different sizes and a variety of tips. Keeping a selection of markers with small,

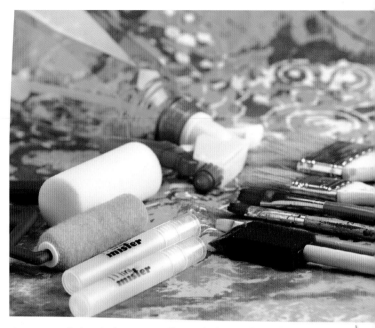

An array of simple but versatile tools for surface design.

medium, and large tips on hand will make the creative process easy.

PAINTBRUSHES

I use paintbrushes to apply paint and dye and always keep a variety of different sizes on hand. I have never treated my brushes very well, so most of the time I purchase inexpensive synthetic brushes in medium to large sizes for painting large surfaces and applying washes of color. I also buy inexpensive sponge brushes to use with stencils or for larger surface areas. I invest in better-quality small brushes made of natural fibers for painting details and patterns.

Pens and markers of all kinds are essential for creating pattern on fabric.

PAINT ROLLER/BRAYER

A paint roller or brayer is a great tool to have on hand, and you'll find that it's useful in a variety of different ways. I use a brayer for the monotype technique shown on page 56.

X-ACTO KNIFE

An X-Acto knife is readily available in any art supply or craft supply store; it has a short, sharp blade that's easy to replace and is a favorite of many designers and crafters for things like cutting stencils or anywhere a clean or precision cut is needed. You can use an X-Acto knife for cutting cardboard but may need to go through the cut more than once. Be sure to use an X-Acto knife on a good cutting surface, such as a self-healing cutting mat, also available in any craft or art supply store.

HOT GLUE GUN

A hot glue gun is a wonderful tool to keep on hand when creating just about any project. I use a low-temperature glue gun when working with fabric and fabric embellishments, such as the fabric flower that decorates the Bucket Hat project, shown on page 134 and in the DVD included with this book.

IRON

You have many choices when selecting an iron to use in sewing projects. I prefer my vintage General Electric iron that my grandmother gave me. It gets very hot and is easy to clean, which makes it perfect for working with fabric that has been painted or dyed. When selecting an iron to use for the projects in *Sew Wild*, I recommend an iron with basic low to high settings that you're willing to get a little dirty.

Use an iron that can get a little dirty for surface design techniques.

SPRAY BOTTLES

Spray bottles in a variety of sizes are a must-have in surface design projects. Fill with water, dye, paint, or even bleach, and create a variety of unique techniques and textures on fabric. (Remember to use safety precautions when working with bleach.)

Surface Design Materials

I use every possible combination of paints, inks, dyes, and markers to add color to fabric and an array of glues, mediums, and bleach to remove or resist color. Together, these processes of adding and removing color add up to endless possibilities for creating beautiful, bright, one-of-a-kind fabrics that you can tear up, rearrange, and stitch up into fabulous projects.

Use water-based dyes, paints, and inks to create an infinite variety of designs and surfaces.

PAINTS AND INKS

I use several different kinds of paints and inks in the techniques in this book and often mix them together. All are water-based, so you can easily clean brushes and applicators (and your hands) with soap and water, and they'll dry quickly. Here are the types of paint and ink that I use most often.

Acrylic paint is versatile and can be used in a variety of fabric and surface design projects. I prefer to use inexpensive acrylic craft paint when creating backgrounds of solid or messy color or things that will get covered up or layered. I will invest in higher quality paint with better color saturation when I am working on surface details. There are a number of different brands, and I always recommend experimenting with inexpensive paint as you are learning and finding your way with new techniques. As you become comfortable, seek out the quality and brand of paint that best suit your needs. You'll find acrylic paint in both bottles and tubes, and both are fine for the techniques in this book. Acrylic paints may change the hand, or feel, of the fabric, stiffening it somewhat, unless diluted or used with a medium made for fabric; if you want to keep a soft hand, use fabric or textile paints.

Fabric or textile paints are best if you're creating wearable items and things that will be washed. I like to use fabric paint the same way that I use acrylic paint—I blend, mix different colors, layer, and experiment with surface design techniques. As with acrylic paint, you'll find an array of colors and finishes, even metallic and pearlized, that you can use to create vibrant surfaces. Often fabric paint has specific heat-setting and washing instructions that vary by brand. Pay close attention to care instructions and try not to mix different brands.

Screenprinting inks can be used with screens, stencils, and masks, or as a substitute for paint. Be sure to look for water-based inks and inks made for use on fabric.

Dimensional paints, also called puff paints, are surprisingly versatile. Most dimensional paints come in a tube with a fine applicator tip that you can use to draw, doodle, and create a variety of details and effects on surfaces.

DYE

While paints sit on top of the fibers in a piece of fabric, dyes actually bond with the fibers, so the hand of the fabric won't change and the dyed fabric can be washed. I enjoy using dye when I'm working with resist techniques and when I want to create a fluid or watercolor-like look and feel in my surface design. There are many options with dye, from all-purpose one-step dyes such as Rit to dyes made for specific fibers that require chemicals and mordants for the dye process. For the techniques and projects in *Sew Wild*, I've used, and recommend, simple one-step dyes that are bottled and ready to use or just need cold water added; these dyes will work well on most natural fibers and even some synthetics. Different dyes also have specific heat setting and washing instructions, so pay attention to these instructions before starting a project.

Bleach, glue, and mediums discharge or resist color; these products work in tandem with dyes and paints to create pattern and design.

BLEACH, GLUE, AND MEDIUMS

Bleach, glue, and art mediums are products that can take away color or resist color by preventing paint or dye from adhering to the fabric. All of these products are inexpensive and readily available; I reach for these products all the time to create pattern and alter surfaces on recycled fabrics or in combination with paints, inks, and dyes.

Liquid chlorine bleach, a widely available household product, chemically removes color from previously dyed fabric. Bleach is a caustic substance; when working with bleach, always work outside or in a ventilated area, wear a mask, and wear gloves. Be sure to rinse the fabric completely when you've achieved the look you want.

All-purpose glue is an easy and affordable material that I use to create a resist pattern on fabric (see page 50). It dries fast, is easy to wash out, and the applicator tip on most bottles is the perfect shape for drawing fine lines and details. Elmer's is a popular and inexpensive brand.

Mod Podge is a water-based acrylic sealer and glue typically used for decoupage projects, but you can also use it to create an easy silkscreen design, as shown on page 60.

Gel medium is a clear water-based binder made for use with acrylic paints; it can also be used to create an easy silkscreen. Gel medium comes in gloss and matte finishes; either one will work for making a screen, but if you're using it as a final sealer on a collage project, you might have a preference.

Stitching Tools

There are many wonderful sewing tools with a lot of bells and whistles available, but you'll need only basic tools for the techniques and projects in *Sew Wild*. I believe in simple, good-quality supplies that will go a long way in different projects. Start with simplicity, and as you become more comfortable and inspired with wild and expressive sewing, begin to experiment with new and different tools.

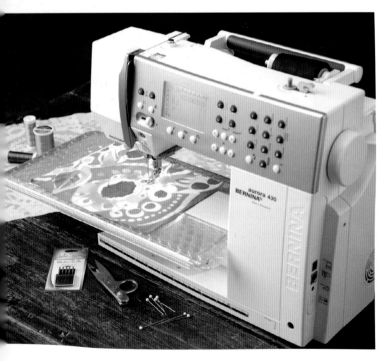

A sewing machine is one of my favorite design tools.

SEWING MACHINE

A good-quality sewing machine will make a world of difference in your sewing projects. For the techniques in this book, you will need a machine with the ability to make straight and zigzag stitches. For free-motion stitching, you'll also want to be able to lower the feed dog; this is as simple as flipping a switch or pushing a button on most modern sewing machines, so check your owner's manual. I work on a Bernina Aurora 430 and love the quality, ease, and the many features that are available, but you can use any machine with these basic capacities.

You may want to experiment with whatever presser feet you have on hand for your machine, but the techniques and projects in *Sew Wild* only require two different sewing machine presser feet: a basic or universal foot for straight and zigzag stitching and a darning or free-motion foot.

Basic presser foot with an opening that allows for both zigzag and straight stitching will hold your fabric in place as you sew.

Darning or free-motion foot combined with lowering the feed dog on your machine gives you the ability to sew in any direction, back and forth and all around. While there are a variety of free-motion feet available, I am still most comfortable using my darning foot for free-motion sewing.

MACHINE SEWING NEEDLES

Keep a range of sewing machine needles on hand at all times. Paper and other nontraditional materials may dull needles very quickly, so change your needle often. It's important to use the correct needle size; too small a needle may break on heavier materials. If you plan to sew with knits, such as the Cozy Jersey Scarf project on page 130, look for ball-point needles designated for knit fabrics.

These are my recommended needle sizes:

» *Light fabrics and paper:* size 8 to 10
» *Medium-weight fabric and materials:* size 11 to 14
» *Fabric or canvas with layers of paint, thick cardboard, heavy materials:* size 16 to 19

HANDSEWING NEEDLES

Most of the projects in this book are made entirely by machine, but a few use handstitching to close an opening or attach a decorative element. You may also want to add handstitching as an expressive touch to some projects. A small book of handsewing needles in a mix of types and sizes will come in handy.

THIMBLE

A metal or leather thimble is useful when handsewing heavy fabric, canvas, or cardboard; it will protect your fingers and help ease the needle through the fabric.

SCISSORS

I have many pairs of scissors, and I tend to use whichever pair is at hand to cut any of the materials I use, whether fabric or paper. Some people prefer to have a separate pair of fabric shears that are used only on fabric (paper will dull scissors quickly) and another

Basic sewing tools and materials will allow you to make all of the projects in this book.

pair of utility or paper scissors for paper. It's really up to you, but make sure you have scissors that fit your hand and are comfortable for you to use.

ROTARY CUTTER AND CUTTING MAT

You can also cut fabric and trim scraps using a rotary cutter and self-healing cutting mat, available in fabric and craft stores. A cutting mat with ruled gridlines and a clear acrylic ruler allow you to cut fabric to a desired size easily.

PINS

I use straight pins to hold down scraps after I've arranged them on a surface and to pin seams for machine stitching.

Sewing Materials

When it comes to sewing, I'm always looking for new ways to use simple things, to put my twist on basic materials, and to create on a budget. Fabrics that you've painted, printed, and altered yourself can be the starting point for an infinite variety of sewn projects, and you can learn to "draw" with your sewing machine and colorful threads to add even more texture and pattern as you go.

THREAD

I use thread to draw, write, and create pattern and texture, so it's important for me to have an assortment of different colors, fibers, and weights on hand. It's always a good idea to envision the project that you'll be creating and pick threads that will meet your needs. There are a number of beautiful thread choices that come in a variety of vibrant colors, made from different fibers and available in different weights.

Typically, I use an all-purpose cotton or polyester thread for most of my projects, but adjust when working on heavy-duty or very light surfaces or when I want to add extra embellishment. Here are some of the choices you'll find in the thread aisle:

» **Cotton** thread is an all-purpose thread available in a variety of colors. It works well on light- to medium-weight cotton, linen, and rayon fabrics. Cotton thread is ideal for handquilting and machine quilting.

» **Polyester** thread is also an all-purpose choice and is great for sewing on most fabrics. It works well on natural-fiber fabrics as well as synthetic fabrics, knits, and stretch fabrics. Polyester or cotton-wrapped polyester is best for utility stitches—the seams that hold your garment or project together—because of its strength, but it doesn't have the brilliance of rayon, silk, or metallic thread.

» **Cotton-wrapped polyester** thread is the most readily available and inexpensive option in most stores; you can use it on most fabrics.

» **Silk** thread is very fine yet strong; it's appropriate for thin fabric or delicately woven fabric. Silk thread has some give and will work well with fabric that has stretch to it. It has a beautiful sheen and costs more than cotton, polyester, or blends.

» **Rayon** thread is glossy and available in brilliant colors; it's designed for machine embroidery and can be very effective for visible stitching of fabric scraps, writing letters or text in thread, quilting layers, and embellishing fabric.

» **Metallic** thread is available for both machine and hand embroidery and is great to use for embellishment.

I often begin with plain white cotton broadcloth or found fabrics and recycled fabrics.

If you do a lot of stitching, as I do, buy your favorite colors on large spools or cones (make sure they'll fit on your machine's spindle) to save money. Look for sales and buy different types and brands of thread to test on various fabrics.

FABRIC

Most of the fabric I use in this book is plain white cotton broadcloth. It's affordable and easy to dye and paint. I also like to use unbleached muslin, canvas, recycled fabrics from my scrap bin, pieces of old clothing, and sheets and tablecloths that would otherwise get donated. I don't normally prewash or dry my foundation fabrics, since most of my painted and altered fabrics won't be machine washed, but if you're in the habit of prewashing, it won't hurt and will help remove any sizing from new fabric.

Art supply stores and textile art suppliers sell fabric marked as Prepared For Dyeing (PFD). These fabrics have no sizing or other chemical enhancements, and you can dye and paint them with great results. I prefer to use whatever's least expensive and most available, but for a special project, you might want to experiment with PFD fabrics.

STABILIZERS

A layer of interfacing, batting, or fleece beneath your fabric, or sandwiched between two layers of fabric, acts as a stabilizer to prevent wrinkles and puckering as you stitch. You don't have to use a stabilizer for your fabric, but it can make life much easier when doing free-motion sewing and creating layers of fabric in nontraditional ways.

Different products will give different results. Fleece adds a soft, thin layer of padding, while batting can add a layer of thin or lofty padding, depending on the fiber. Interfacing adds some stiffness—the amount depends on the type and weight of interfacing. It's best to try different stabilizers to familiarize yourself with the effects of each. Some general guidelines follow:

» **Fusible interfacing** has an adhesive on one side that is activated by the heat of an iron. It comes in weights from very light to heavy, and you'll find black or white in some types. Most fusible interfacings are synthetic fibers, while a few are cotton. All will bond to fabric when ironed. This product can make life really easy. I use fusible interfacing to arrange and attach lots of small scraps and pieces before quilting. Start with a medium-weight all-purpose fusible interfacing that's inexpensive and readily available at craft and fabric stores.

» **Sew-in interfacing** adds body but must be sewn to the fabric; it has no adhesive. It's also available in a range of weights. These products are very effective for stability when free-motion writing or drawing with thread.

» **Batting** is traditionally used as the middle layer of a quilt. I like to use batting for the inside of handbags or as a stabilizer for free-motion stitching; the batting gives the fabric a quilted appearance. Batting is available by the yard or in precut sizes and in different fibers and blends. Cotton batting is great for beginners and small projects; it's thin and requires stitching that is more closely spaced than polyester batting. Polyester batting is lightweight and inexpensive; it's good for art quilts and projects that won't be washed. It packs well and will add puffiness to your projects. Wool batting is very warm, absorbs moisture, and is a good choice for a quilt that you'll use on a bed.

» **Fleece** is similar to batting, but a bit thinner, and it's a great choice when you want an inexpensive stabilizer without bulk. Fleece is available by the yard or in packages. You don't need to worry about how closely spaced your stitching is when using fleece.

Alternative materials such as photographs, book pages, and packaging add texture to your surfaces.

ALTERNATIVE MATERIALS

Who says you have to limit your sewing to fabric? There are alternative materials that you can easily stitch through, combining them with fabric or using them on their own, such as lightweight cardboard packaging, colorful plastic bags, and scraps of wrapping paper. Once you start using these materials, you'll find yourself looking at everything through a designer's eye and recycling many things into materials for sewing projects. Look for bold graphics and interesting text, colors, and textures.

Sewing through these materials will dull your needle quickly, so you'll want to change to a new needle when you switch back to sewing fabric. Make sure your needle is large enough to penetrate your materials and sew carefully while you adjust to the difference between fabric and other items. When sewing lightweight metal, be very careful; wear safety glasses and go slowly.

Here are some of my favorite alternative materials:
» Paper
» Book and magazine pages
» Junk mail
» Lightweight cardboard, plain or corrugated
» Plastic and paper bags
» Rope
» Yarn, ribbon, thread, and lace
» Wrapping paper
» Wallpaper
» Old letters and photographs
» Food and cereal boxes and labels
» Lightweight metal

MAKE A SIMPLE SWATCH JOURNAL

I COLLECT A LOT OF INSPIRATION: color swatches, pieces of all my handpainted fabric, inspirational textures and patterns, and just about anything that I might want to reference in future projects. I create simple fabric books to store all of my swatch inspiration and then sew all of my inspiration to each page over time. This journal is easy to make and could be altered to fit a variety of different themes and projects. These instructions result in a journal that's about 7¼" x 11" (18.5 x 28 cm) when closed.

1 Quilt fabric scraps to an 11" x 14" (28 x 35.5 cm) piece of batting. Add a layer of backing and binding if desired. Fold the finished small quilt in half to make the outside of the book.

2 Fold about 20 fabric scraps and paper pieces in half to create pages. You can make them uniform by starting with 11" x 14" (28 x 35.5 cm) pieces or vary the sizes.

3 Lay the fabric scraps and paper pieces on top of the inside of the book, lining up the folds of each piece with the fold in the book cover.

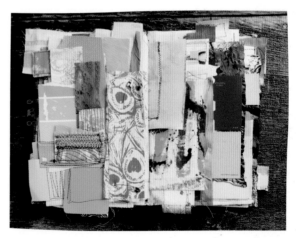

4 Using the sewing machine, sew straight down the fold through all layers with a zigzag stitch. This is the spine of your journal.

5 Now you can start adding content. Use the sewing machine or handstitching to sew inspiration swatches of fabric or paper to the pages.

6 Organize the pages by color themes, patterns, and textures. Create tabs on the pages to separate the themes.

COLOR, PATTERN, AND InSpiRatIon

AT THE HEART OF EVERYTHING I CREATE is a passion for color and pattern, and I make it a daily challenge to learn about and understand these concepts. It's become a ritual in my life to study different color combinations and schemes, use them in my work, and to always be on the lookout for inspiration. I also look for and discover pattern everywhere; as you begin to explore color and pattern together, you'll find endless possibilities for making fantastic fabric.

Color

Color is always by my side, challenging me, inspiring me to grow as an artist, and keeping me on my toes. While much of my process is impulsive and expressive, I am very intentional with my use of color. I believe that a good understanding of basic color theory makes all the difference in any creative project. While color theory takes some time to learn, it is important to practice, understand, and work with the fundamentals.

The first color theory class that I took in college bored me to tears. I was already passionate about color and went in thinking it would be exciting, creative, and an easy A. I came out confused, uninspired, and barely passing the class. It took me years of additional classes and actual practice to finally start to appreciate that it takes more than passion to understand and work with color—it takes time and discipline.

In some ways, color theory is more like math or science than art. There are combinations, rules, and formulas for how it all works. Without an understanding of this information, creative projects can look drab, muddy, or lacking in visual harmony. While I struggled through (and bombed) that first class, I have never once regretted the experience and the awareness that it brought to my creative life.

These days, while I don't get too concerned with complex formulas and details, I do rely on the simple basics of color theory. Whether you are just getting started with color, looking to grow, or want a better understanding, the basics and simple color schemes are a great place to start and practice using color. Here are some basics to help you get started.

COLOR WHEEL

The color wheel is an important visual tool in understanding color and color relationships. I like to keep a color wheel accessible when creating. Many art supply stores sell color wheels, or you can even create your own from fabric, paint, or scraps of colorful paper.

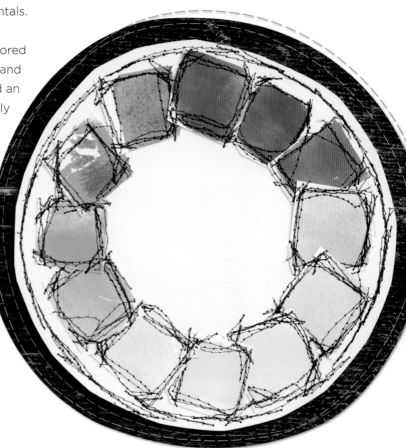

Make your own color wheel from scraps of fabric or painted paper.

Cool colors (top row) and warm colors (bottom row).

Primary colors.

Secondary colors.

Tertiary colors.

WARM AND COOL COLORS

The color wheel can be divided in half: one side has cool colors (green, blue, purple), and the other side has warm colors (yellow, orange, red). Warm colors are energetic and vibrant, while cool colors can be calm and peaceful.

PRIMARY COLORS

In traditional color theory, red, yellow, and blue are primary colors—the three colors that are the basis for all of the other colors. You can mix these primary colors in different ways to create all the other colors on the color wheel.

SECONDARY COLORS

Green, orange, and purple are secondary colors; you'll find them in between the primary colors on the color wheel. Mix secondary colors using the primary colors that surround them on the color wheel; for example, mix red and yellow to make orange.

TERTIARY COLORS

These are the colors formed by mixing a primary and secondary color: yellow-orange, red-orange, red-violet, blue-violet, blue-green, and yellow-green.

Color Harmonies

Color harmonies are arrangements of color or schemes that are pleasing to the eye. They engage the viewer and create a natural sense of order and balance. When color is not in harmony, it can be boring, chaotic, or just not look right. There are all kinds of color harmonies and specific formulas for creating visual interest with color. Here are few of the most basic and commonly used schemes.

MONOCHROMATIC

A monochromatic color scheme uses only one color in different shades or tints. This is one of my favorite color schemes to use because, while simple, it can create balance and harmony and is pleasing to the eye.

This monochromatic color scheme uses a range of tints and shades of red.

An analogous color scheme creates visual harmony in a patterned surface.

Complementary colors create high visual contrast.

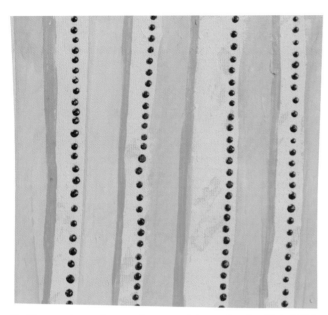

Split complementary colors provide contrast without the inherent tension of complementary colors.

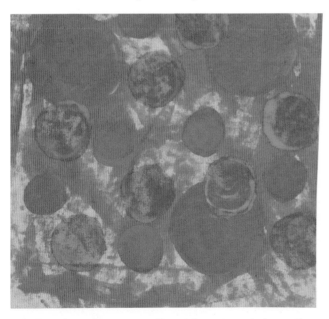

Triadic color schemes are vibrant by nature; balance the elements carefully.

ANALOGOUS

An analogous color scheme uses three (or more) colors that are next to each other on the color wheel. This scheme is often found in nature, and like a monochromatic scheme, also has a way of creating a visual harmony. Try using one color as the dominant color to create contrast. An analogous color scheme is effective when filling a surface with a busy pattern.

COMPLEMENTARY

Complementary colors are opposite each other on the color wheel. Their relationship to each other often produces visual tension, but can also make each color appear brighter by creating visual contrast. While complementary colors are considered the least harmonious, a palette using complements can be harmonized by adding a neutral color. I love using complements when I want to establish high contrast in a project.

SPLIT COMPLEMENTARY

A split complementary scheme incorporates one dominant color and the two colors that are on either side of its opposite on the color wheel. This scheme is great for high contrast without the visual tension of complementary colors.

TRIADIC

A triadic color scheme uses colors that are evenly spaced around the color wheel. Triadic color schemes tend to be quite vibrant, even if you use pale or unsaturated versions of your hues. To use a triadic harmony successfully, the colors should be carefully balanced. Let one color dominate the scheme and use the two others for accent.

TIPS FOR EXPLORING COLOR

After you understand simple color theory and schemes, challenge yourself to continue learning and trying new ways to explore and incorporate color in your daily routine. Here are some of my favorite ideas for color exercises and exploration.

» **Take a little time for research.** Build on the basics by challenging yourself to learn more complex theory. There are a number of books and websites that will bring you up to speed (see Recommended Reading, page 142).

» **Keep a color journal,** dedicated to color observation and reflection. This is a wonderful way to build up resources and palette ideas and a way to be more intentional when working with color. Carry this journal everywhere you go, adding swatches of color and color combinations. Collect scraps of paper, photos, fabrics, and paint chips in colors that you like and add them to your journal.

» **Pay close attention** to the colors that you respond to, photos that pop, fashion that you love. Record your findings in your color journal. How does a color combo make you feel? What makes you notice certain colors? How could you incorporate those colors into you work?

» **Pay attention to the colors** that you use in your work and make note of your discoveries. Build a color palette from your favorite photos.

» **Look for color inspiration** in your surroundings. Snap photos of places and things that have colors that catch your eye.

» **Develop a few favorite go-to palettes.** Put together a color board with your favorite palettes that you can utilize when you're in a pinch, or when you need to get going on a project but don't want to spend time trying to pick colors.

» **Be aware.** Take note of the colors that attract you. Reflect upon why you choose certain colors, what catches your eye, how it makes you feel, and what the colors express.

» **Try limiting your color palette** and put your focus and creative energy on one color. Pick one color and use different shades and tones to create visual interest or use related colors with one strong unrelated accent color.

» **Maintain contrast.** Find different ways to create contrast to create a visual push and pull.

» **Make a statement.** Experiment with how your color choices reflect your message.

» **Let your instincts take over.** Instead of thinking too much, try experimenting with only using instinct. Quickly grab colors to work with and challenge yourself to create without too much thought. Pay attention to the end result—did it work? Do you like it? Continue to work on using instinct instead of overthinking your color choices.

» **Repeat color** to create pattern or use large areas of color to create visual interest and draw attention to different shapes.

» **Love your colors.** Be passionate about the colors and color combinations that you use. Focus on these combos and explore them thoroughly, then try adding pops of new color to your favorite combos.

Try limiting your color palette to one color with variations.

Pattern

There is nothing that I love more than a surface full of pattern. There are numerous ways to fill a surface with pattern and repetition, but I prefer drawing. With a background in fine art, I am most comfortable with a pen in hand and a blank surface to fill. Drawing—and even doodling—is the simplest and purest process you can incorporate into your daily creative routine. For some reason it has always reminded me of running: you can take it anywhere, it is free, simple, requires lots of discipline, doesn't always feel good, and the more time you spend doing it the better you get.

I always keep a sketchbook on hand—in fact, I keep one in my purse, one in my studio, and one beside my bed. Whenever an idea strikes, I make sure to draw it in the pages of one of these sketchbooks. I use these drawings as a starting point when designing and creating my patterns on fabric.

Drawing and doodling come easily to some people, but not everyone is comfortable with the process. Keep at it, and with a little time and discipline you'll become more at ease with the process of drawing and building pattern.

TIPS FOR EXPLORING PATTERN

» **Look for inspiration.** Fabric, wallpaper, clothing, textiles, nature, and everyday things are great sources of pattern ideas.

» **Reserve a sketchbook,** and a pen, pencil, or marker for drawing—no writing or art journaling, just drawing. Use this sketchbook as a place to develop pattern ideas.

» **Make time** to draw and doodle. Take ten minutes a day to experiment on paper.

» **Start small and simple.** Pick shapes that are easy to draw. Some of the most graphic and pleasing patterns are based on simple circles, triangles, dots, or squares.

» **Use simple lines** and details to fill in and around shapes.

» **Repeat a shape** over and over again, varying the size and details.

» **Experiment with shading,** use of light and dark, thick and thin lines. Don't let yourself be too concerned with being perfect; focus on being expressive. Let go and enjoy the process.

» **Try filling an entire page** with doodles and shapes and drawings, going all the way to the edge. This is great practice for working on fabric.

» **Pick a section** from one of your drawings that you like best and repeat it to develop a pattern. You can even make multiple photocopies of your chosen section of drawing and then arrange and rearrange them.

HOW TO Develop A Pattern

1. To begin, I select a motif from a doodle or drawing and start experimenting.

2. I draw it in different sizes, rotate it, and overlap motifs.

When I am happy with the overall look and feel I use my experimental sketches as a reference and start creating my fabric.

3. I add shading, details, and color.

4. I play with different sizes and variations.

Photos by Alisa Burke

OVER THE YEARS I HAVE DEVELOPED a lot of creative habits, traditions, and rituals. The most important of these is the way that I seek out inspiration and ideas. I don't typically struggle with creative blocks or feeling uninspired, but I do find that in order to evolve and grow as an artist I have to develop challenges for myself.

These days I spend very little time looking for inspiration online. Instead, I get far away from the computer and out of my art studio. I go outside, into my community, and look for ideas. I pack up my camera and a sketchbook and set out to find just about anything that sparks an idea. I often assign myself creative tasks that are centered around one subject, color, texture, or pattern.

When I am at home in California and not on the road teaching, I take mini field trips every week to what I call my "go-to places." These include about ten locations that are a ten- or fifteen-minute walk or drive from my house, and they're places where I know I will always find a variety of color, texture, design, and inspiration. I alternate my favorite places each week—a park, the zoo, the beach, a construction site, a flower stand.

When I am on the road traveling, which ends up being quite a lot, I always have a camera on hand. I'm constantly snapping photos, taking notes, and sketching anything and everything that catches my eye. The result of this ritual is a digital library full of photos that I can pull from for inspiration, pages of sketches and doodles that get transformed into pattern, and inspiration that is

100 percent authentic for my lifestyle. The photos at right and on page 30 are a few of my inspiration images.

Regardless of where you live, by the beach, on a farm, big city or small town, there is inspiration everywhere. Find a couple of your own go-to places where you can count on finding inspiration that you can incorporate into your work.

Here are a few more places to visit to stimulate your creative energy and get your brain going!

- » farmer's markets
- » city streets
- » local architecture
- » junkyards
- » rolling hills
- » mountains
- » community parks
- » fabric stores
- » the mall
- » lakes, rivers, and streams
- » galleries and museums
- » subways and buses
- » art supply stores
- » bookstores
- » grocery stores
- » forests
- » desert landscapes
- » garden centers
- » your own backyard

SURFACE DESIGN
TECHNIQUES

I ALMOST NEVER BUY PRINTED FABRIC because I know how easy it is to make my own. Surface design techniques are the quickest way to transform plain fabric. Since I have a background in painting, I am naturally drawn to using color, texture, and the concept of simple layering to create unique surfaces. These concepts can also be applied to sewing projects. In this section, we will explore some of my favorite surface design techniques; use them by themselves or in different combinations to create layers. My hope is that these techniques will inspire you to think outside of the box with materials and surfaces.

Doodling and Drawing

WHAT YOU'LL NEED:

Plain light-colored woven fabric

Fine-point permanent marker

DOODLING AND DRAWING are quick and easy ways to create unique patterned surfaces. You don't have to be an artist or even be good at drawing—simple shapes, marks, and designs can be used in repetition to create a surface full of pattern. The more comfortable you become, the more you can begin to add complexity to the shapes and pattern. Look for patterns in daily life that inspire you, doodle and draw shapes and objects that come naturally to you, and experiment with a variety of different pens and tools.

1. Start with a blank surface. Select a shape to draw that is comfortable and easy to execute freehand. Use a preliminary sketch for reference if needed.

2. Begin by drawing a doodle in the center of the surface **(fig. 1)**.

3. Add details, marks, and shading **(fig. 2)**.

4. Add more of the same doodle in different sizes **(fig. 3)**.

5. Continue to add more details, marks, and shading so all of the doodles begin to create a pattern Repeat the doodles over and over again, letting them overlap and blend together **(fig. 4)**.

6. Work your way across the entire surface until it is full **(fig. 5)**.

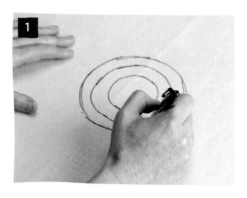

» Go wiLD

Doodle with paint and brush; doodle with dye and brush; doodle with dimensional fabric paint (puff paint).

Freewriting, Lettering, and Text

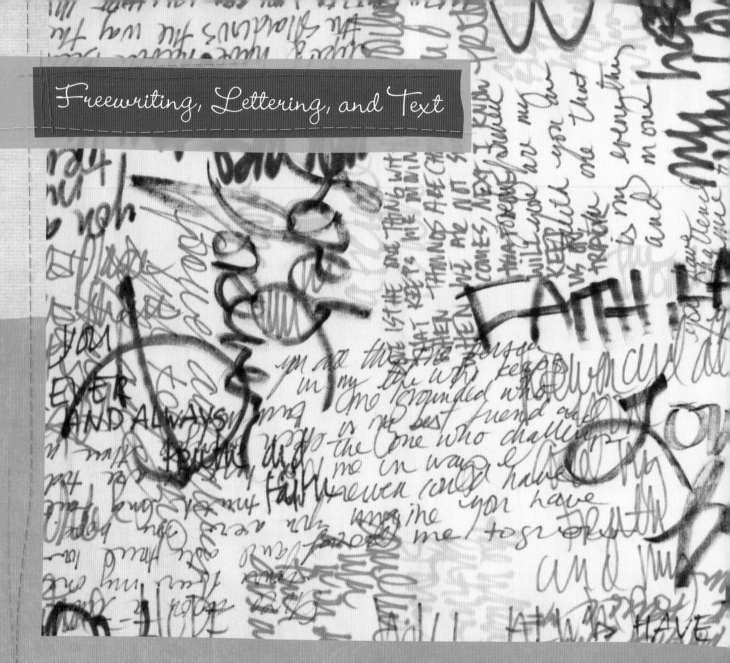

WHAT YOU'LL NEED:

Plain light-colored woven fabric or paper

Assorted markers

USE WRITING, WORDS, AND TEXT to create an interesting surface full of texture and pattern. Freewriting is simple. You can do it with any number of different tools and variations. It instantly adds a personal element and is just about the easiest way to fill a surface.

1. Start with a blank surface. Use permanent markers or fabric markers and begin freewriting **(fig. 1)**.

2. Fill the surface with personal thoughts, experiences, or even your favorite quote or lyrics. Treat the surface as your journal **(fig. 2)**. For variation, rotate the surface as you write.

3. Use different colors **(fig. 3)**.

4. Use different sizes of lettering **(fig. 4)**.

5. Use different styles of lettering **(fig. 5)**.

6. Work your way across the entire surface until is it full **(fig. 6)**.

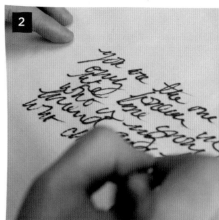

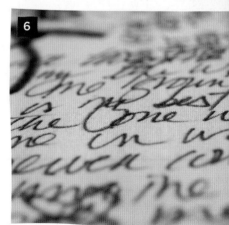

Graffiti-Style Letters

WHAT YOU'LL NEED:

Plain light-colored woven fabric

Acrylic paint in one color and white

Pencil

Thick markers in one color and black

Paintbrush

I LOVE TO INCORPORATE DIFFERENT STYLES of lettering into surface design, and some of my favorite inspiration comes from graffiti. Graffiti letters come in all sizes and shapes; they can be tangled, unreadable, wild, and even cute. I've found the easiest way to begin creating graffiti letters is to start with balloon-style lettering and then move on to experimenting with different styles.

1 Begin by picking a simple word. Sketch your word in light pencil on the fabric, letting the letters touch and overlap each other. Outline the letters with a thick marker **(fig. 1)**.

2 Using the thick marker, highlight one side of each letter; this will begin to add extra dimension **(fig. 2)**.

3 Mix acrylic paint in the color of your choice with a little white acrylic paint. Using a paintbrush, fill the letters with color **(fig. 3)**.

4 Mix white paint to create different shades, working your way from dark to light in each of the letters **(figs. 4 and 5)**. Fill in all of the letters with color **(fig. 6)**.

5 Use the paint to add a wash of color around the word **(fig. 7)**.

6 Finish by outlining the word with black marker for even more contrast **(fig. 8)**.

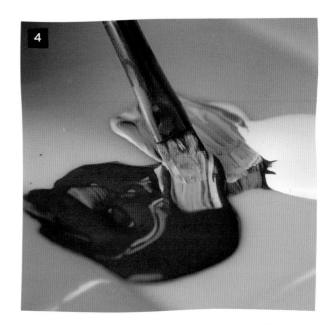

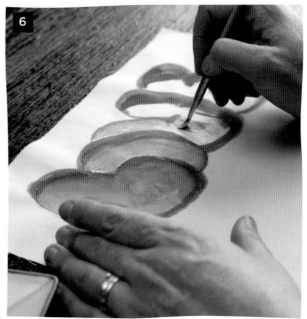

⌃ Go wiLD

Top row, from left: Write at an angle; scribbling or obscure writing; outlined letters.

Row 2: Stenciled letters; stamped letters; expressive cursive.

Row 3: Letters with doodling on the outside; letters filled with solid color; letters with solid-color background.

Row 4: Experiment with size and shape.

Building Layers of Color with Paint

what you'll need:

Plain light-colored woven fabric
Acrylic paints in three colors
Paintbrush

THE EASIEST WAY to create vibrant and colorful fabric is with layers of paint or dye. Applying two or three colors quickly and expressively produces a simple but striking surface that you can use in a variety of projects. I'm using acrylic paint in the how-to photographs on page 43, but you can also use textile paint or dye; if needed, heat-set according to manufacturer's instructions.

1. Select two colors. Begin by brushing one color onto the surface of the fabric **(fig. 1)**.

2. Add the second color and brush onto the surface **(fig. 2)**.

3. Keep your brushstrokes quick and expressive **(fig. 3)**.

4. Blend the edges of the colors in some areas **(fig. 4)**.

5. Cover the entire surface with color **(fig. 5)**. Let dry.

6. Add a third color with quick swipes, letting the first layer of color show through **(fig. 6)**.

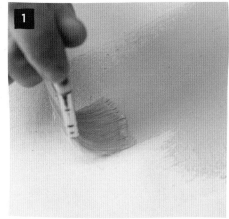

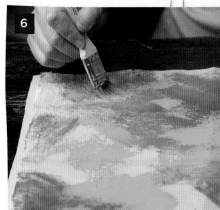

Wet-on-Wet Painting

WHAT YOU'LL NEED:

Plain light-colored woven fabric
Acrylic paints in several colors
Spray bottle filled with water
Paintbrushes

WET-ON-WET IS A PAINTING TECHNIQUE in which pigment is applied to a wet surface, resulting in soft watery marks and color. I love to apply this technique to fabric painting. It's a perfect way to create light, airy, and pretty fabric.

1. Start by wetting down the entire surface of fabric with a spray bottle filled with water **(fig. 1)**.

2. Dip a brush in paint or dye and apply to the wet surface **(fig. 2)**.

3. Fill the surface with simple shapes or patterns, letting areas of color bleed and blur **(fig. 3)**.

4. Create contrast by going back over existing shapes with paint **(fig. 4)**.

5. Work your way along the surface. If the wet surface starts to dry, use the spray bottle to rewet **(fig. 5)**.

6. Continue to cover the surface until it is filled with color and shape **(fig. 6)**.

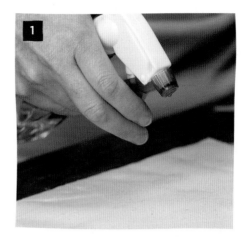

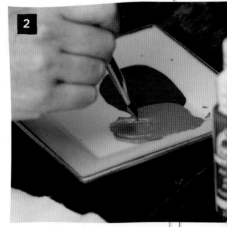

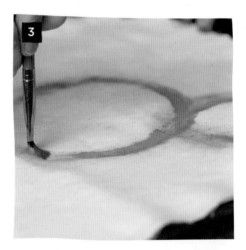

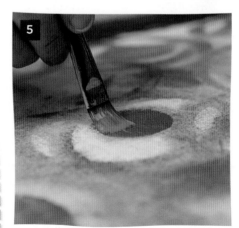

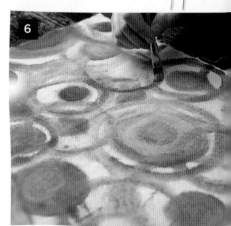

Woodblock Printing

WHAT YOU'LL NEED:

Sketch of your design

Pencil

Piece of wood for carving, any size (see note)

Wood-carving tools

Acrylic paints

Paintbrush or roller to apply paint

Plastic or glass palette or plate for rolling out paint or ink

Fabric or surface to print on

Optional: Hammer or mallet

note: *When selecting wood for carving, note that woods with tighter grain are easier to carve. Hardwoods can be challenging to carve but will hold fine details, while soft woods are easier to carve but not good for details. Maple is an economical choice. Craft supply stores often sell carving or whittling blocks that work well for beginners.*

ONE OF MY FAVORITE WAYS to create printed fabric is by carving my own simple woodblocks, inspired by the ancient craft of block printing by hand. Wood carving takes a little practice and some patience, but once you get the hang of it, it's well worth the effort to print your own one-of-a-kind fabric. If you're not up for the challenge of wood carving, try using a linoleum block, which is a little softer and easier to carve.

1 Start with a fresh piece of wood. In pencil, draw the design onto the surface of the wood **(fig. 1)**.

2 Use wood-carving tools to carve away the design. The areas that you carve away will be the negative space, or the areas that will not print. Start with the large portions and save the small details for last **(figs. 2 and 3)**.

3   When you are satisfied with the carved pattern, apply paint or ink to the carved side of the wood with either a brush or a roller **(fig. 4)**.

4   Press the woodblock, carved side down, firmly onto the surface of the fabric. For a cleaner image, use a hammer or mallet and pound on the back of the block, taking care to keep the block steady **(fig. 5)**.

5   Carefully pull the block from the fabric **(fig. 6)**.

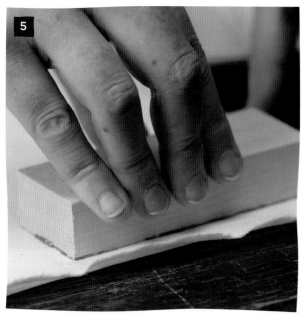

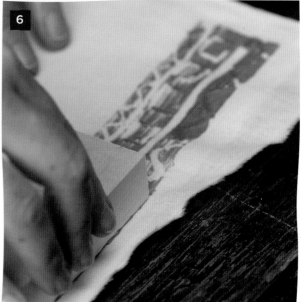

6   Repeat the pattern along the surface **(fig. 7)**.

7   Alternate the direction of the woodblock for variation in the pattern **(fig. 8)**.

8   Incorporate a second design in a different color for contrast and variation **(fig. 9)**.

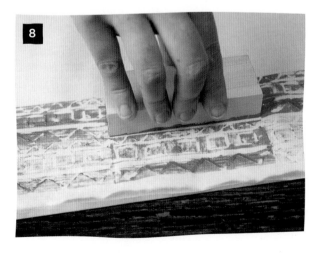

Creating Pattern with Glue Resist

WHAT YOU'LL NEED:

Plain light-colored woven fabric

Water-based glue such as Elmer's

Fabric dye or fabric paint

Paintbrushes

A RESIST IS A METHOD THAT PREVENTS dye or paint from reaching fabric and is often used to create pattern. While there are different resist methods, including wax, paste, or even chemicals, I prefer using glue resist. It is a simple, clean, and an affordable way to create a rich and interesting surface. When choosing fabric, consider how bright you want your finished fabric to be; different fabrics show color differently.

1 Lay fabric on a flat surface. Using a bottle of water-based glue as a drawing tool, squeeze glue from the bottle and draw a design on the surface of the fabric **(fig. 1)**. Remember that wherever you apply glue the fabric will not absorb color.

2 Repeat the design over and over again. Cover the entire surface, adding detail as you go. Let dry completely.

3 Use paint or dye and cover the entire surface with color. You can either dip your fabric in a dyebath or apply with a brush **(fig. 2)**. Follow the manufacturers' recommendations for setting the dye or paint.

4 Wash and dry the fabric. The glue will have washed away, and you will be left with a beautiful pattern **(fig. 3)**.

Tip If you don't have any dyes at hand, try diluted acrylic paint, screenprinting ink, or coffee or tea for a natural stain.

≽ Go wiLD

Top row, from left: Brushstroke with glue; leaf imprint with glue.

Row 2: Stamp with glue; bubble-wrap imprint with glue.

Row 3: Writing with glue, toilet paper roll imprint with glue.

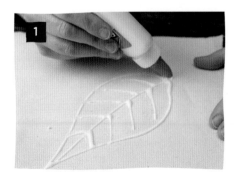

Discharging with Bleach and Adding Color with Paint or Dye

WHAT YOU'LL NEED:

Dyed fabric or recycled fabric with a color or print

Gloves

Mask

Household liquid bleach

Inexpensive synthetic paintbrush for bleach

Dye, textile paints, or acrylic paints to add layers

Paintbrush for dye or paints

SAFETY PRECAUTIONS!

Wear gloves when working with bleach.

Work outside or in a well-ventilated area and/or wear a mask.

Keep in mind that bleach can damage materials; use synthetic paintbrushes (bleach will quickly eat away a natural-fiber brush).

DISCHARGE IS THE PROCESS OF REMOVING COLOR from fabric, and household bleach is the most familiar and easily accessible discharging agent. With discharging, you can create pattern, lettering, or expressive marks. Bleach is strong and has the potential to damage and eat away both synthetic and natural fibers. You can make a solution as weak as two tablespoons of bleach per cup of water all the way up to full-strength bleach. I use full-strength bleach on cotton fabric, but I always recommend testing results on different fabrics before getting started.

1 Lay your fabric on a flat, protected surface. Put on gloves and mask.

2 Use a brush dipped in bleach to mark, draw, or letter on the fabric **(figs. 1 and 2)**.

3 Let the fabric sit and allow the bleach to develop, but don't allow it to eat through the fibers **(fig. 3)**.

4 When your designs appear and the desired color has been pulled from the surface, wash thoroughly and let dry **(fig. 4)**.

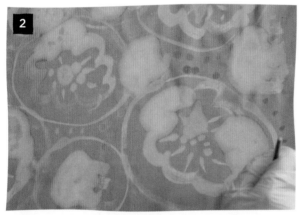

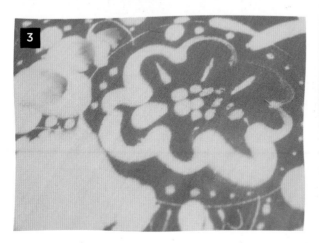

5   Once your discharged fabric is dry, you can go back into the surface with dye, textile paint, or acrylic paint. Add lines, details, and color to the entire surface **(figs. 5, 6, 7)**. Set dyes or paints as needed.

Tip *Even after bleach is washed from the fabric, it can still eat away the fiber. In addition to rinsing the fabric, you can also use a product such as Bleach Stop, Anti-Chlor, or even hydrogen peroxide to neutralize after bleaching.*

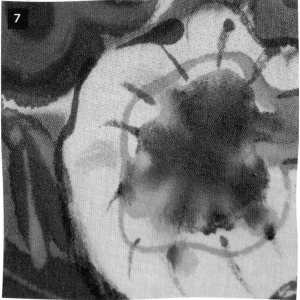

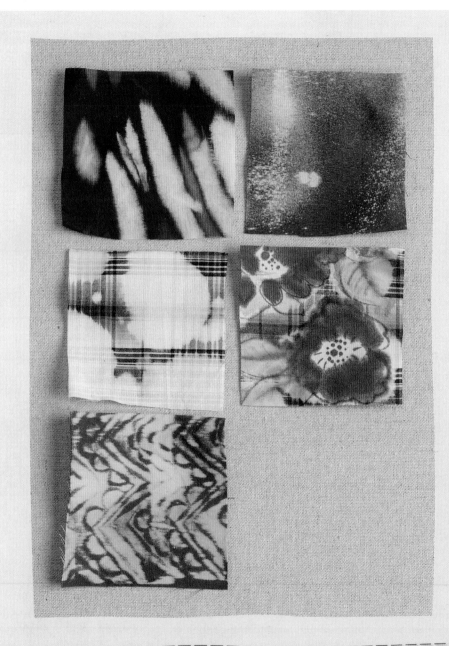

« Go wiLD

Top row, from left: Stencil with bleach; splattered bleach.

Row 2: Bleach on recycled fabric; paint added to bleached surface.

Row 3: Stamping with bleach.

Monotype Printing

WHAT YOU'LL NEED:

Plexiglas sheet in a size to accommodate your design

Screenprinting ink or fabric paint

Brayer

Cotton swabs

Paintbrushes

Rags

Plain light-colored woven fabric to print on

A MONOTYPE (not to be confused with a monoprint) is a process of printmaking that involves drawing or painting with ink or paint on a smooth, nonabsorbent surface or printing plate. The instructions that follow describe inking the entire surface of the plate, pulling the ink away with rags, and then transferring or printing the plate onto another surface. You can also create a monotype by painting a design onto the plate and then transferring the design onto another surface. A monotype produces a lovely image or pattern that is expressive, painterly, and one-of-a-kind.

1 Lay the piece of Plexiglas on a flat, protected surface.

2 Using the brayer, cover the entire surface with screenprinting ink **(fig. 1)**.

3 Using cotton swabs, rags, and brushes, begin to draw into the ink, pulling the ink away from the surface **(fig. 2)**.

4 Continue to pull ink away to create a surface filled with images or pattern **(figs. 3 and 4)**. When the entire printing plate is covered in pattern, set it aside.

5   Lay your fabric on a flat surface. Gently pick up
    the Plexiglas plate from the bottom **(fig. 5)**.

6   Carefully flip over the Plexiglas and place the
    inked or painted side on top of the fabric **(fig. 6)**.

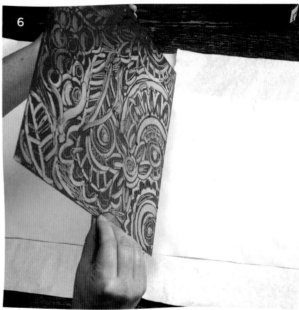

7   Press down firmly **(fig. 7)**.

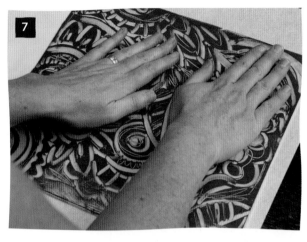

8   Pull the plate up slowly, letting the fabric peel away **(fig. 8)**.

9   If you like, you can often transfer one additional print, called a ghost, which will be much lighter than the original **(fig. 9)**.

Easy Screenprinting with Embroidery Hoop or Picture Frame

WHAT YOU'LL NEED:

Two-part wooden embroidery hoop

Mesh fabric for screen

Pencil

Paintbrushes

Gel medium

Plain light-colored woven fabric to print on

Screenprinting ink or textile paint

Stiff cardboard or old credit card to apply ink

SCREENPRINTING IS A GREAT WAY to create one-of-a-kind fabric, but it can be time-consuming and messy. Making your own screen from an inexpensive wooden embroidery hoop is just about the easiest way to create a screenprinted image or design that can be used over and over again. When I'm short on time and money, I employ these easy methods that have been floating around the crafting world for a while.

1 Separate the two parts of the hoop. Stretch
   the mesh fabric over the inner hoop. Place
   the outer hoop back onto the inner hoop and
   tighten the screw to hold the fabric in place
   (fig. 1). Pull fabric taut.

2 If you have an image that you want to trace,
   place the image beneath the hoop with flat
   side of hoop down **(fig. 2)**.

3 Use a pencil or pen to draw your pattern or
   image on the mesh **(fig. 3)**.

4 Once the design is finished, use gel medium
   to paint over all of the negative spaces of the
   pattern (in other words, no color will print
   wherever you've applied gel medium) **(fig. 4)**.
   Allow the gel medium to dry.

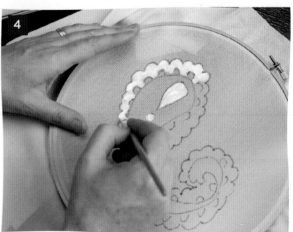

5   Lay fabric on a flat surface and place the screen facedown. Squirt screenprinting ink or fabric paint onto the surface of the screen at the top of the pattern **(fig. 5)**.

6   Using a piece of stiff cardboard or an old credit card, wipe the ink or paint down and across the mesh surface of the screen **(fig. 6)**.

7   Carefully pull the screen away from the fabric **(fig. 7)**.

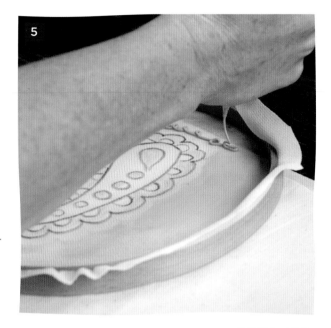

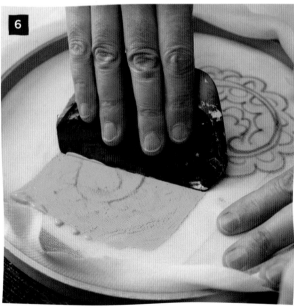

8   Repeat across the entire surface
    to create a pattern **(fig. 8)**.

9   When the ink or paint is dry,
    heat-set it according to the
    manufacturer's directions, if
    needed.

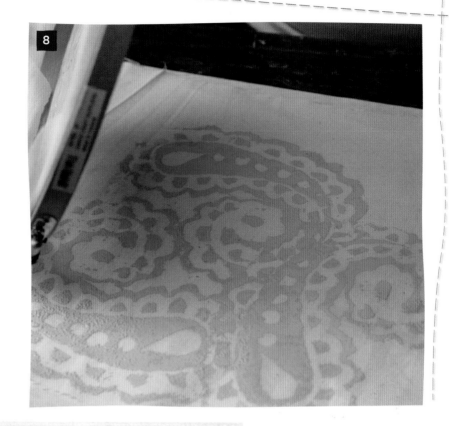

Variation:
PICTURE FRAME SCREENPRINTING

You can also use a picture frame to make an inexpensive frame for
screenprinting; a larger frame allows for a larger screen and more
pattern. Just remove the glass and lay the frame on a flat surface. Trim
mesh fabric to the size of the frame plus an additional 1" to 2" (2.5 to
5 cm) on all sides. Staple the sides of the mesh to the frame, pulling the
mesh as taut as possible. Create your pattern and print as above.

Stenciling

WHAT YOU'LL NEED:

Plain light-colored woven fabric

Stencil, either handmade
(see note) or purchased

Paintbrushes

Textile paint or dye

note: *It's easy to create your own stencil to save money and make use of materials you probably have on hand. Try using cardstock, an old file folder, or a scrap of lightweight cardboard as stencil material; just use an X-Acto knife to cut away a shape or design, leaving open space that can be filled with color.*

STENCILING ALLOWS YOU TO CREATE DESIGNS made up of open spaces through which paint or ink will transfer. While it's common to associate stencils with spray painting, they are just as easy to use with paint or even dye applied with a brush. Repeating a stenciled image across your fabric is a very quick and easy way to create a pattern.

1 Lay fabric on a flat surface. Place your stencil on top of the surface (tape down the sides if you are concerned about your stencil moving around). Dip your brush in paint or dye and lightly dab over the top of the stencil **(fig. 1)**.

2 Lift the stencil up carefully. Replace stencil on a new section of fabric and repeat paint or dye application.

3 Repeat until you have the entire surface filled with pattern **(fig. 2)**.

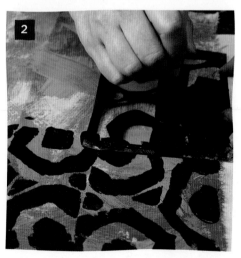

⌄ Go wiLD

Top row, from left: Stencil used as a stamp; mask over recycled fabric.

Row 2: Stencils layered in different colors; stencil over recycled fabric.

Row 3: Stencil with fabric dye printed in light and dark variations to create the look of shadows.

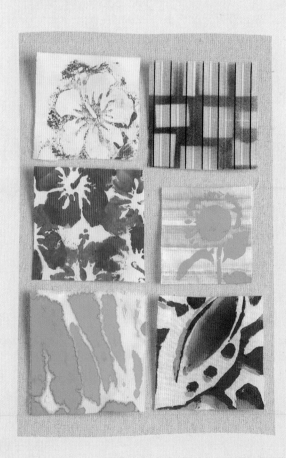

Masking

WHAT YOU'LL NEED:

Woven fabric

Mask in your desired shape (I use a mask cut from sturdy paper, such as an old file folder)

Spray bottle filled with dye or paintbrush

Textile paint or dye

A MASK IS A LITTLE DIFFERENT FROM A STENCIL. The mask prevents color from transferring wherever the mask is placed. Use a mask to add texture and pattern to your surface or use it as you make a second or third layer of pattern to protect areas of pattern or color that you want to keep.

1. Lay fabric on a flat surface. Place your mask on top of the surface. **Fig. 1** shows a discharged fabric, and I use the mask to protect an area that I want to keep as is.

2. Use a spray bottle filled with dye or a paintbrush and paint or dye to cover the surface with color **(fig. 2)**.

3. Lift up and move the mask and repeat until you are satisfied with the surface **(fig. 3)**.

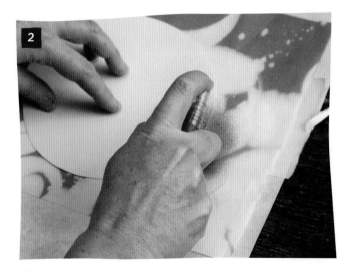

Fusing Plastic

WHAT YOU'LL NEED:

Four to six recycled plastic bags
(I like to use Target* bags)

Scissors

Iron and ironing board

Two pieces of scrap fabric as large
as the bags

* Target Corporation is not a sponsor
  of this project and is not affiliated
  with Sew Wild, Alisa Burke, or
  Interweave.

PLASTIC BAGS ARE EASY to transform with heat. When fused together, they create a versatile and strong surface that you can paint, alter, and use in mixed-media and sewing projects. With a few simple steps, you will be on your way to creating unique material to use in variety of projects. Be sure to work in a ventilated space and go slowly and carefully until you know how fast the plastic will fuse without melting.

1 Begin by collecting four to six plastic bags. Cut the bottoms and the handles off of the bags and discard **(fig. 1)**.

2 Stack the bags on top of each other **(fig. 2)**.

3 Smooth out the wrinkles and place the stack of bags on top of a large piece of scrap fabric **(fig. 3)**.

4 Place another piece of scrap fabric on top of the stack **(fig. 4)**.

5 With the iron on a low setting, press slowly back and forth across the surface **(fig. 5)**.

6 Once the plastic is fused, remove the layers of scrap fabric. Your fused plastic is ready to stitch or paint.

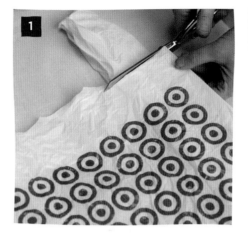

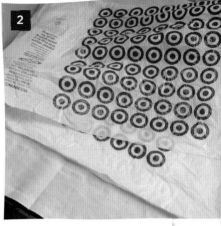

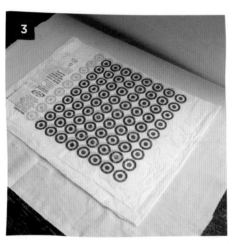

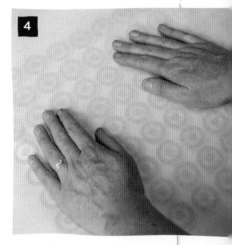

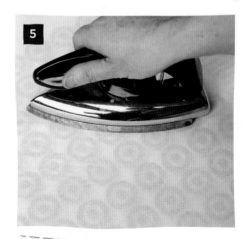

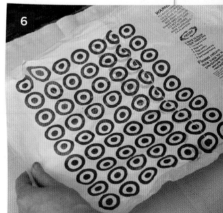

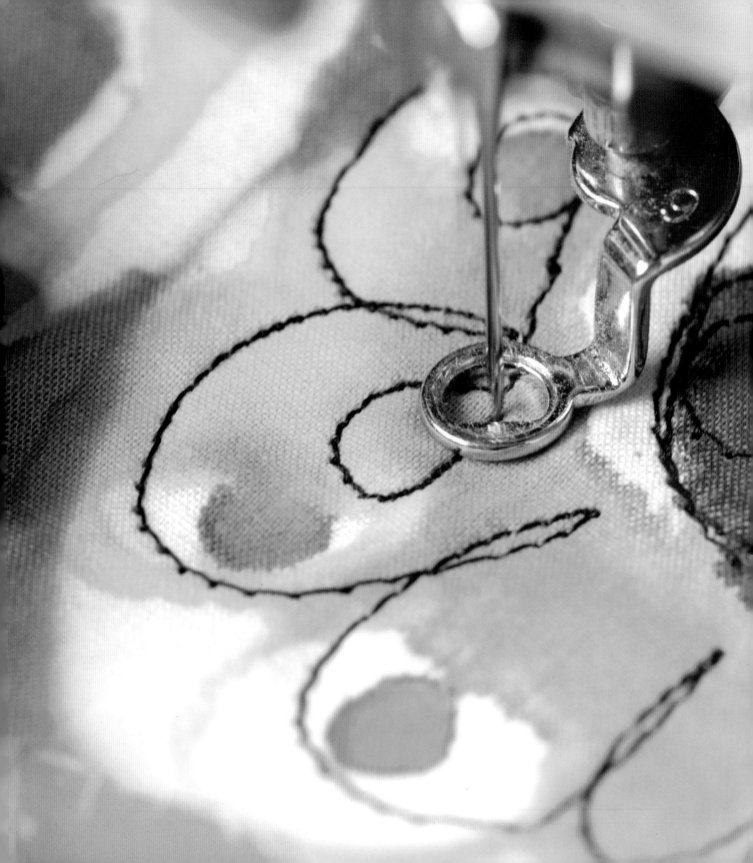

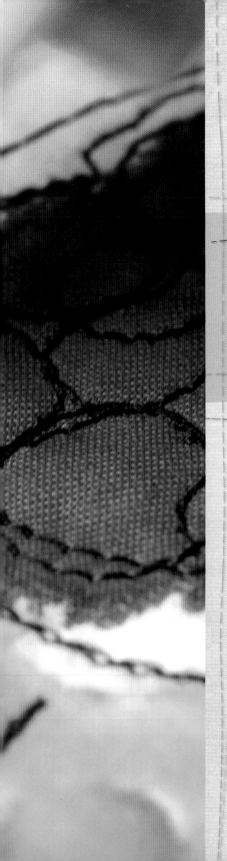

STITCHING TECHNIQUES

In this section, you won't find a lot of technical terms, rules, or fundamentals. Instead, I share simple and easy ways to get started using the sewing machine as a tool for making marks, establishing line and color, and layering. Be sure to stock up on sewing machine needles in several sizes, so you always have a sharp needle on hand, and sewing machine thread in many colors.

I use basic straight stitching and zigzag stitching when assembling projects, and I make use of free-motion stitching when creating a surface full of texture and layers. I refer to "messy stitching" in many projects. This means having fun and going wild with stitching and not getting caught up in making straight lines and perfect stitching.

Free-Motion Stitching

what you'll need:

Fabric

Sewing machine with lowered feed dog and darning foot

Optional: Fabric stabilizer and/or embroidery hoop

WHILE I USE STANDARD straight stitching and zigzag stitching to create expressive lines, cover raw edges, and create strong contrast, I'm also a big fan of free-motion stitching. The free-motion technique gives you the ability to sew in any direction and in any design. Instead of letting the machine control the direction, as it does with straight or zigzag stitching, attach a darning foot (or free-motion foot), lower the feed dog, and use your hands to move the fabric. Take a look at the DVD included with this book for a live demonstration of free-motion sewing; with just a little practice, you'll find that it's very easy to do.

1 Start by lowering the feed dog on the machine, which will stop the machine from grabbing the fabric from below. **Fig. 1** shows the feed dog in the raised position, and **fig. 2** shows the feed dog lowered. Most machines have a simple switch that lowers the feed dog (consult your owner's manual).

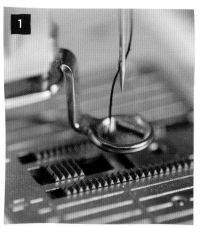 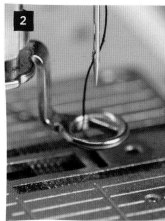

2 Insert your fabric under the needle. If desired, use a layer of fabric stabilizer under the fabric. Some people like to put the fabric in an embroidery hoop and place the hoop flat side down on the machine bed. When you're ready to stitch, place your hands on the fabric, apply light pressure, and slowly move the fabric in the direction you want to go as you use your foot or knee pedal to start stitching *slowly* **(fig. 3)**.

3 For example, if I want to cover the surface with circles, I move the fabric in a circular motion **(fig. 4)**.

Tips

» *Do a lot of experimentation. Work on a variety of different fabrics and surfaces to find what you like best.*

» *Keep a steady speed; try not to speed up and slow down.*

» *Always use fresh, sharp needles.*

» *For a quilted appearance, use batting or interfacing underneath your fabric.*

» *Experiment with different speeds on the machine and slowly work up to getting faster.*

» *Let yourself be messy and free as you experiment.*

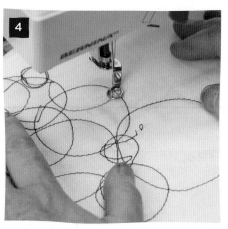

Stitching Over Patterned and Painted Surfaces

ANOTHER WAY TO USE FREE-MOTION STITCHING is to add layers of depth and interest to surfaces that have pattern and designs. This might be your own painted and dyed fabric, as shown here, or fabric that has been purchased or repurposed. Use the machine and free-motion stitching to trace over the patterns and designs on the fabric. Get creative with thread in different colors, contrast, and sheens.

1. Lower the feed dog and place your fabric in the machine **(fig. 1)**.

2. Start in the center and guide your fabric along the surface, outlining the pattern on the surface and adding detail within, making your way around the fabric **(fig. 2)**.

3. Challenge yourself to trace the entire pattern and cover the surface with stitching **(fig. 3)**.

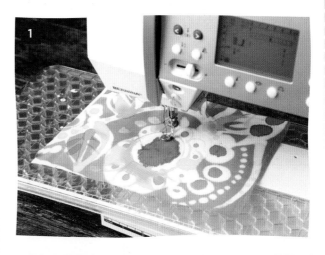

⌃ Go wiLD

Top row, from left: Stitching on recycled fabric; stitching on wallpaper; stitching on hand-dyed fabric.

Row 2: Stitching on purchased fabric; stitching on painted fabric; stitching on bleached and stenciled fabric.

Row 3: Stitching on wrapping paper; stitching on recycled cardboard packaging.

ESTABLISHING LINE, CONTRAST, AND COLOR with STITCHING

USE MACHINE STITCHING to establish line, contrast, and color, and create visual interest with machine and handsewing on your surfaces. Keep simple design concepts in mind to elevate your work to another level.

Top row, _from left:_ _Light and dark colors of thread on contrasting surfaces; different colors of thread; stitched lines of varying weights; thin curvy lines for a peaceful and airy appearance._

Row 2: _Varied sizes of stitched shapes and patterns; only primary colors of thread; expressive zigzag lines for energy and excitement; dark repeating lines for a bold appearance._

Row 3: _Thick and thin lines around shapes and images; different values of one color of thread; stitching outlines of shapes and objects; stitching shades on shapes and objects._

Row 4: _Heavy texture next to light texture; different colors of stitching layered on each other._

Freehand and expressive drawing with stitching

WHEN YOU START TO GET COMFORTABLE with free-motion sewing, you can challenge yourself to get more detailed and expressive by drawing and doodling with the machine. These stitch patterns and designs are beautiful by themselves or can be used as another layer on painted and dyed surfaces.

- » **Practice drawing** your design a few times before starting.
- » **Use patterns, doodles, and designs** that come naturally, then graduate to more challenging detailed drawings.
- » If you are not comfortable drawing your design, *try tracing it* onto your fabric. Use this as a last option; the best part of drawing with the machine is being free and expressive.
- » **Challenge yourself** to let go of perfection and move expressively and freely around the surface.

These six swatches show a simple line drawing progressing to a more complex and detailed drawing.

Journaling and Writing with Machine Stitching

WHAT YOU'LL NEED:

Sewing machine with feed dog that can be lowered and darning foot

Fabric

Optional: Fabric stabilizer and/or embroidery hoop

USE YOUR SEWING MACHINE as a writing tool to create a surface full of visual interest by journaling and freewriting all over your fabric. This technique takes practice and control, but once you have mastered it, it's a beautiful way to incorporate lettering and writing into sewing and quilting projects.

1   Start by lowering the feed dog and place your fabric in the sewing machine. Use a fabric stabilizer and/or embroidery hoop if desired. Start at one side and work your way across the surface, moving your fabric to create letters and words **(fig. 1)**.

2   Continue to write across the surface of the fabric with stitching **(fig. 2)**.

3   Instead of picking up the needle in between letters and words, keep your needle in the fabric and create a line to connect the elements **(fig. 3)**.

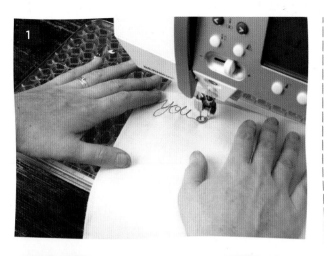

Tips

» *Cursive writing works best for free-motion writing. Have fun with exaggerated loops and shapes of cursive letters.*

» *Try varying the size of the letters and words.*

» *Experiment with different colors of thread on different-colored surfaces.*

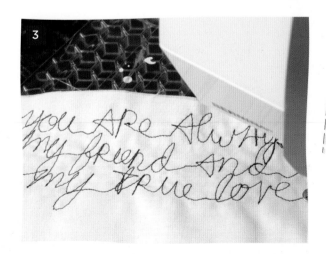

sewing WITH ALTERNATIVE MATERIALS

WHILE I LOVE FABRIC, I also enjoy experimenting with stitching on different materials. In my opinion, just about anything can be stitched. I often dig through the trash and recycling bin for materials that would be interesting to use in my sewing. Stay on the lookout for unique materials with interesting color, pattern, and texture. Cut, rip, and redefine things that would typically get overlooked. Once you start to feel comfortable using the sewing machine with expressive stitching and free-motion sewing, you can begin to experiment with using alternative materials in sewing projects.

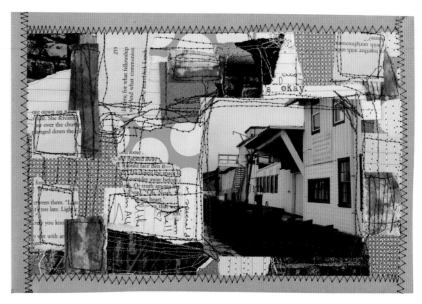

Make simple stitched collages of alternative materials backed and bound with plain paper and frame them or send them in the mail.

Top row, from left: Shape cut from fabric; flower cut from fabric; paint over patterned fabric.

Row 2: Lace; dyed fabric; lace.

Row 3: Recycled bandanna; ribbon.

Top row, from left:
Wallpaper; wrapping paper.

Row 2: Fused plastic bags; recycled envelope.

Row 3: Thin metal or aluminum foil; map.

Top row, from left:
Stitching on book page; stitching on corrugated cardboard.

Row 2: Stitching on brown paper bag; stitching on cardboard.

Row 3: Stitching on map; stitching on photograph.

Top row, from left:
Cardboard food box; book pages.

Row 2: Junk mail; paper bag.

Row 3: Magazine page; index card.

Top row, from left:
Stitching on recycled greeting card; stitching on fused plastic bags.

Row 2: Stitching photograph onto fabric; stitching on fused plastic bags.

Row 3: Stitching on metal; stitching metal on recycled greeting card.

Building Stitched Layers

WHAT YOU'LL NEED:

Plain or painted, dyed, or printed fabric for background

Scraps of fabric and alternative materials

Pins or fusible web

Sewing machine

THERE IS NOTHING MORE BEAUTIFUL than a surface filled with layers of color and texture. Regardless of the technique I'm using, I am always looking for ways to establish the look and feel of layers by combining different techniques and materials on top of each other. With this technique, you can easily mix alternative materials, such as photographs, with fabric.

1   Select a fabric for the background. Select bits and pieces of fabric and alternative materials that you want to incorporate into the surface **(fig. 1)**.

2   Create a rough layout for the placement of your fabric and materials **(fig. 2)**.

3   Pin pieces to the surface or use a fusible web to secure fabric to the background **(fig. 3)**.

4   Use stitching to sew along the edges and within the pieces, as desired **(fig. 4)**. You can use straight stitching, zigzag, or free-motion stitching.

5   Add smaller pieces on top of the large pieces and to fill in small spaces **(fig. 5)**.

6   Vary your stitching to add interest and texture **(fig. 6)**.

7   Continue to add layers on top of layers until you are satisfied with the surface **(fig. 7)**.

Variation:
QUILTED LAYERS

To use this technique and create a surface with a quilted look and texture, first baste a quilt "sandwich" with a piece of fabric as the top layer, a layer of batting in the middle, and a bottom layer of fabric for the backing. Baste with loose handstitches or pins. Repeat the steps above for the layers and surface design. While layering, keep in mind the concept of contrast: layer light on top of dark to create a visual push and pull between layers. Keep your color scheme in mind and stick to it. Experiment with different shapes and sizes of fabric layered on top of each other.

Adding a layer of batting and a backing fabric gives your piece a quilted appearance.

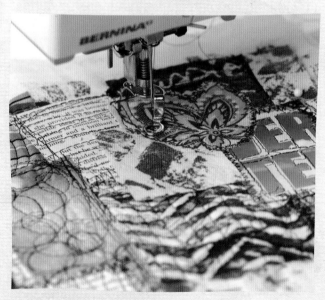

Stitching the quilted layers.

Graffiti Quilting

what you'll need:

- Fabric that you've painted or dyed with colorful words
- Sharp sewing or embroidery scissors
- Plain or layered fabric for foundation
- Pieces of scrap fabric
- Sewing machine with darning foot
- *Optional:* Fabric stabilizer or a layer of batting and fabric for backing

MUCH OF MY CREATIVE INSPIRATION comes from graffiti and the concept of layering text, words, and colors. I've applied this inspiration to my sewing and quilting projects and have discovered a way to create fabric graffiti using layers of colorful fabric, expressive stitching, and bold appliquéd letters, for unique and fresh results.

1 Select fabric that has been covered in color, words, and text **(fig. 1)**.

2 Use the scissors to cut out words and pieces of text and lettering **(fig. 2)**.

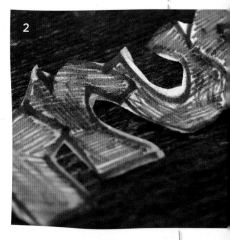

3 Place the cut-out words on a foundation of plain or layered fabric **(fig. 3)**. Begin to stitch the words to the foundation.

4 Use stitching to create visual interest and texture **(fig. 4)**.

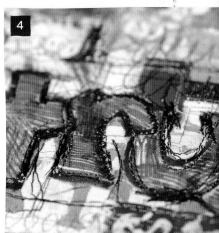

5 Continue to add layers on top of layers with a focus on lots of text and words **(fig. 5)**.

Tips

» *Let bottom layers show through.*

» *Experiment with adding shading to the letters with paint.*

» *Don't trim threads and frayed edges; let them remain on the surface as textural elements.*

PROJECTS

NOW THAT WE'VE EXPLORED COLOR, pattern, sources of inspiration, and all of my favorite surface design and stitching techniques, it's time to put it all together. This is your chance to go wild and use your imagination to the fullest. Layer and combine all the techniques you've learned in any way that strikes you; print over painted backgrounds, discharge recycled fabrics and then add color with printing and dyes, create patterns with permanent markers or glue resists, combine and layer scraps of fabric and use messy stitching to attach them to a base fabric or a layer of batting, add found cardboard or photographs to fabric in a creative mix of alternative materials.

Practice all of the surface design and stitching techniques in the previous chapters, singly or in combination, until you have a good selection of printed, patterned, painted, layered, and stitched fabric pieces to work with. Watch the DVD included with this book to help you along. Then, with the fabric you've created, start sewing the projects that follow. These easy-to-make projects will help you get wild with your own sewing. You'll find that you now have the creative tools to make almost anything you can imagine.

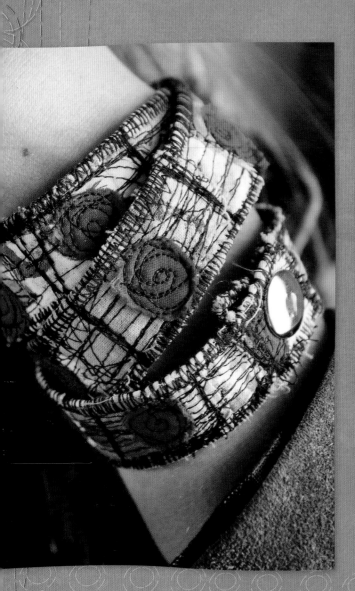

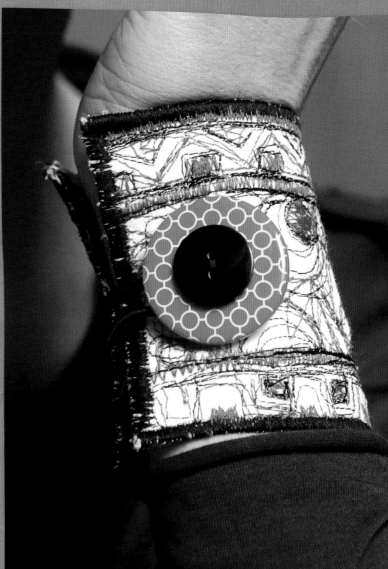

WONDER WOMAN
CUFF BRACELETS AND FLOWER STRAP BRACELET

THE POSSIBILITIES FOR CREATING BRACELETS out of your own handmade fabric are endless. Messy stitches, lines, text, and free-motion stitching make for beautiful, textural, expressive accessories. Wear them individually or in combination for a dramatic effect.

FINISHED SIZES

Green and purple cuff:
3½" x 7½" (9 x 19 cm) plus elastic

Red, black, and white cuff: 3" x 6½" (7.5 x 16.5 cm) plus elastic

Multicolored strap bracelet with red flowers:
1" x 23" (2.5 x 58.5 cm)

MATERIALS

For cuffs:
9½" x 8" (24 x 20.5 cm) of white cotton or linen fabric
13" x 8" (33 x 20.5 cm) sew-in interfacing or stabilizer
3½" x 8" (9 x 20.5 cm) fabric for backing
Decorative button
2½" (6.5 cm) elastic cord
Thread in desired colors

For strap bracelet:
2" x 23" (5 x 58.5 cm) sew-in interfacing or stabilizer
Small fabric scraps in varying sizes and colors
Dritz Heavy Duty Snap in size 24 or other ⅝" (1.6 cm) diameter 4-part no-sew heavy-duty snap fastener
Thread in desired colors

TOOLS

Fabric scissors
Pins
Sewing machine
For strap bracelet: Dritz Jumbo Snap Tools to attach no-sew snap fastener

To make the cuff bracelet:

1 Cut the white fabric into two pieces, one 3½" x 8" (9 x 20.5 cm) and the second 6" x 8" (15 x 20.5 cm).

2 Cut the interfacing into two 3½" x 8" (9 x 20.5 cm) pieces and one 6" x 8" (15 x 20.5 cm) piece.

3 Place the 6" x 8" (15 x 20.5 cm) piece of fabric on top of the same-size piece of interfacing or stabilizer.

4 Using free-motion stitching, fill the fabric with stitched lines and patterns, messy shapes, and writing.

5 After the surface is filled, cut the stitched fabric into four to six strips.

6 Arrange the strips of stitched fabric on a 3½" x 8" (9 x 20.5 cm) piece of interfacing. Play with different variations and ways to arrange the strips. Set aside any leftover strips or fabric scraps for another project.

7 When satisfied with the arrangement, sew each of the strips down to the interfacing with more messy stitches. Use a zigzag stitch to cover the raw edges of the strips.

8 Sew a decorative button onto one end of the cuff.

9 Stitch the backing fabric onto the remaining piece of interfacing. Use straight and zigzag stitches to cover the surface.

10 Stack the front and the back of the cuff together, with right sides out.

11 Using a closely spaced zigzag stitch, stitch through all layers along two long edges and the button edge.

12 Loop the piece of elastic cord and place it between the two layers of the open short edge of the cuff. Sew the edge down with a closely spaced zigzag stitch, securing the elastic as you go.

To make the strap bracelet:

1 Cut a strip of interfacing 1″ x 23″ (5 x 58.5 cm) or long enough to wrap around your wrist three times.

2 Using a variety of scraps, cover the surface of the interfacing with scraps. When you're satisfied with the arrangement, sew the scraps down with lots of messy stitching.

3 Fold the strip in half lengthwise and press lightly. Stitch around all four edges of the folded strap with a closely spaced zigzag stitch.

4 Stitch some small bright contrasting circles of fabric at regular intervals along the strap (mine are spaced about 1½″ to 1¾″ [3.8 to 4.5 cm] apart). Fill each circle with stitched details to create the look of flowers.

5 Using the snap tool as directed on the package, insert a heavy-duty snap on each side of the bracelet.

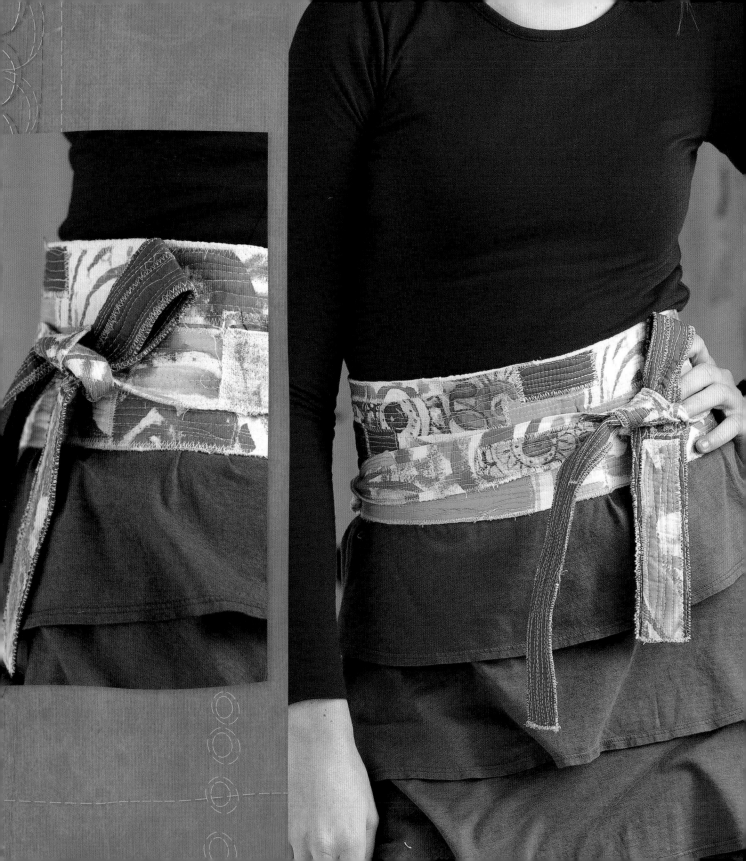

OBI-STYLE
WRAP BELT

THIS UNIQUE BELT IS A PERFECT WAY to define your waistline and add a burst of color to your look. Inspired by the obi, a Japanese sash traditionally worn with kimono, and made from fabric scraps, this quick and simple project can be modified in shape and color to reflect your personal style. Vary the width of the belt to suit your proportions and choose colors that make you feel exotic and beautiful.

FINISHED SIZE

40" x 4½" (101.5 x 11.5 cm) plus 1¾" x 28" (4.5 x 71 cm) ties on each side, to fit waists from 26" to 30" (66 to 76 cm).

MATERIALS

1½ yd (137 cm) of 45" (114.5 cm) wide cotton or linen fabric for main belt fabric and ties (this fabric will show on wrong side of belt and ties)

1½ yd (137 cm) fleece or thin batting

Scraps of painted and altered fabric in a variety of shapes, sizes, and colors (enough to cover surface of main belt panel and ties)

Thread in desired colors

TOOLS

Fabric scissors

Pins

Sewing machine

schematic

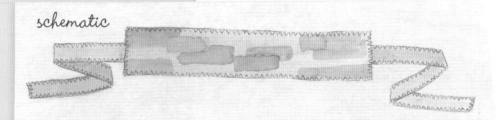

Obi-Style Wrap Belt, back view

1 From the main belt fabric, cut one 40″ x 4½″ (101.5 x 11.5 cm) rectangle for the front panel of the belt and two 28″ x 3½″ (71 x 9 cm) rectangles for the side ties (you may adjust the length or width of the front panel as needed). Repeat for fleece or thin batting.

2 Make the side ties. Lay one 28″ x 3½″ (71 x 9 cm) tie in main belt fabric wrong side up. Smooth fleece or batting of same size on top. Begin to lay out your fabric scraps over the surface of the batting, alternating color and pattern for variation. When you're satisfied with your arrangement, pin the scraps in place through all layers.

3 Sew the scraps down, sewing through all layers with lots of visible messy stitching. Fold tie in half on the long dimension and press lightly.

4 Repeat Steps 2 and 3 for second tie and set ties aside.

5 Lay the belt front panel wrong side up. Smooth batting on top. Arrange scraps on the surface until you're satisfied with the arrangement and pin the scraps down through all layers.

6 Before stitching scraps down, insert the ties between the batting and the fabric rectangle on the bottom, so that about 2″ (5 cm) of each side tie is "sandwiched" into the front panel **(fig. 1)**. Pin in place.

7 Sew the scraps down, sewing through all layers with lots of messy stitching, securing side ties as you stitch.

8 Using a closely spaced zigzag stitch, stitch around all edges of front panel and ties.

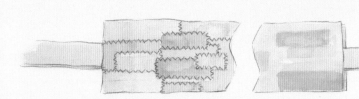

fig.1 *Insert ties between batting and backing.*

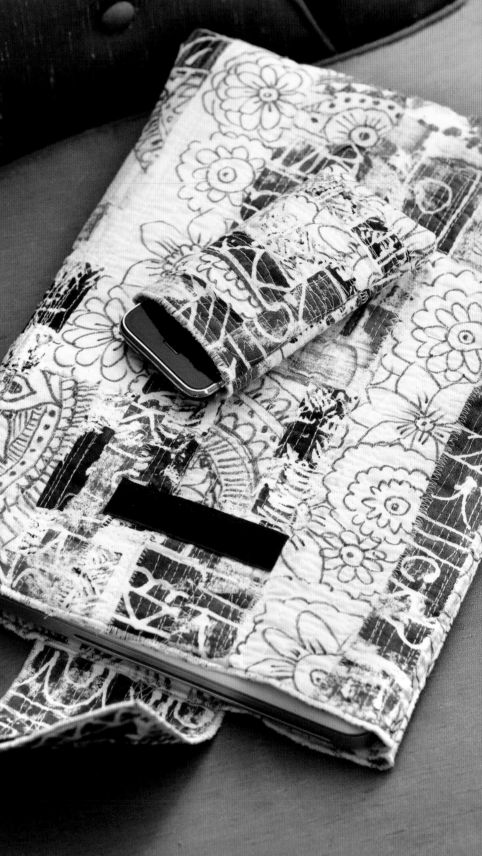

smart AND wild
LAPTOP AND PHONE CASES

MOST OF US TAKE OUR DIGITAL TOOLS with us everywhere these days. Why not sew a cute case with an easy hook-and-loop tape closure to protect your laptop, with a matching case for your iPod or smartphone? I used a black, white, and gray neutral color scheme, but your favorite bright colors would work equally well. Adjust the size to fit your laptop or digital device.

FINISHED SIZES

Laptop cover: 10" x 14" (25.5 x 35.5 cm) to fit a 13" (33 cm) laptop

Phone/iPod case: 5⅛" x 3⅛" (13 x 8 cm)

MATERIALS

For laptop cover:
Painted and altered fabric scraps in a variety of shapes and sizes
18" x 21" (45.5 x 53.5 cm) lightweight fusible interfacing
18" x 21" (45.5 x 53.5 cm) fleece or thin batting
18" x 21" (45.5 x 53.5 cm) lining fabric
3¼" (8.5 cm) of ¼" (2 cm) wide hook-and-loop tape
Thread in desired colors

For iPod or phone case:
Painted and altered fabric scraps
3⅝" x 10¾" (9.25 x 27.5 cm) lightweight fusible interfacing
3⅝" x 10¾" (9.25 x 27.5 cm) fleece or thin batting
3⅝" x 10¾" (9.25 x 27.5 cm) lining fabric
Thread in desired colors

TOOLS

Fabric scissors
Press cloth (generous scrap of muslin or other plain woven fabric)
Iron
Pins
Sewing machine

To make the laptop case:

1. Cut the interfacing into two pieces for the front and back of the laptop case, each 10½" x 14¼" (26.5 x 35.5 cm), and one piece 3¾" x 8¼" (9.5 x 21 cm) for the flap closure. Do the same for the fleece or batting and the lining fabric.

2. Select a variety of painted, printed, and altered fabric scraps in different shapes and sizes, choosing colors and textures that work together.

3. Place one 10½" x 14¼" (26.5 x 35.5 cm) piece of lightweight fusible interfacing with the adhesive side up. Arrange fabric scraps on the surface of the interfacing.

4. When you're satisfied with the arrangement, place a press cloth over the fabric scraps and press with a warm iron to lightly fuse the scraps to the interfacing and hold them in place. Repeat with the second piece of interfacing.

5. Place one piece of interfacing with fused fabric scraps on top of a same-size piece of fleece or batting and pin in place.

6. Begin to machine stitch the scraps in place. Use different kinds of stitching inside of the different fabric sections, use lots of messy stitches along the sides and corners of the scraps, drop the feed dog and have fun adding a layer of free-motion stitching to the surface—be playful and enjoy the process.

7. Repeat the same process for the second piece.

8. Spread out one 10½" x 14¼" (26.5 x 35.5 cm) piece of your lining fabric, wrong side up. Lay one piece of the stitched fabric and batting on top, right side up. Quilt the layers together with a repetitive stitch (straight, doodles, circles, etc.). Repeat for the second panel.

9. Finish one short edge of each piece with a closely spaced zigzag stitch.

10. To create a flap for the closure, take your remaining 3¾" x 8¼" (9.5 x 21 cm) piece of interfacing and repeat the process of attaching scraps, quilting the fused scraps to batting, and stitching to lining fabric. Stitch around all four edges of the flap with a closely spaced zigzag stitch.

11. Center one half of the hook-and-loop tape about 2" (5 cm) from the top (zigzagged edge) of one panel, on the right side. Stitch down. Pin the other half of the hook-and-loop tape to the wrong side of the flap, about ½" (1.3 cm) from one short edge **(fig. 1)**. Stitch down.

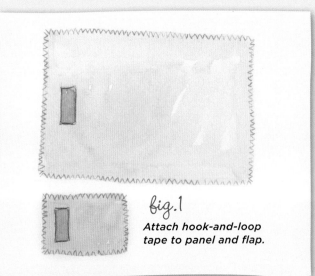

fig.1
Attach hook-and-loop tape to panel and flap.

12 Center the flap on the top edge of the other panel, on the right side, so that half of the flap extends beyond the edge **(fig. 2)**. Sew the flap to the panel around all edges and across the center of the flap.

13 Place the two laptop cover pieces right sides together. Pin and sew sides and bottom with a straight stitch in a ¼" (6 mm) seam. Sew seam allowances together with a zigzag stitch.

14 Turn laptop case right side out. Secure flap by pressing the two hook-and-loop tape strips together.

To make the phone case:

1 Cut interfacing into two pieces, each 3⅝" x 5⅝" (9.25 x 13.75 cm). Repeat with interfacing or batting and lining fabric.

2 Using the same method described for laptop case, fuse scraps of fabric to the interfacing, stitch the fused scraps to batting, and stitch fabric and batting to lining fabric.

3 Finish the top edge of each panel with closely spaced zigzag stitching.

4 Place the two panels right sides together and sew the sides and bottom with straight stitch in a ¼" (6 mm) seam. Stitch the seam allowances together with a zigzag stitch.

5 Turn case right side out.

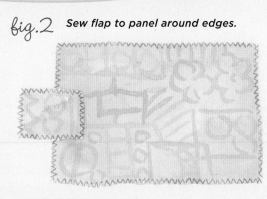

fig.2 *Sew flap to panel around edges.*

ROSETTE
PILLOW

THIS SWEET PILLOW WITH ITS STRONG COLOR and lots of texture will add a little fun to your couch or bed. The project makes good use of colorful fabric scraps; my version has multicolored flowers, but you could also try a version where all the rosettes are in the same color family. I demonstrate the process for making the rosettes on the DVD included with this book.

FINISHED SIZE

10" x 15½" (25.5 x 39.5 cm)

MATERIALS

16" x 21" (40.5 x 53.5 cm) piece of colorful painted fabric for front and back of pillow

10¼" x 16" (26.5 x 40.5 cm) piece of interfacing or thin batting

Scraps of fabric for leaves

Twenty-four fabric rosettes of varying sizes, or as many as desired (see instructions on page 104)

12 ounces (367 g) polyester fiberfill stuffing

Thread in desired colors

TOOLS

Fabric scissors

Pins

Sewing machine

Fabric glue or hot glue gun

Handsewing needle

1 Cut the colorful painted fabric into two pieces, each measuring 10½" x 16" (26.5 x 40.5 cm). Use one piece for the pillow front and set one piece aside for the pillow back.

2 Back the pillow front with the interfacing or batting and use free-motion stitching to stitch simple stems and leaves to the surface.

3 Cut scrap fabric into leaf shapes (the pillow shown has about a dozen leaf shapes, varying from about 1¾" to 2¼" [4.5 to 5.5 cm] long). Use free-motion stitching to attach the leaves randomly along the stems, adding stitching around the leaf shapes and within, to suggest the veins of the leaves.

4 Make rolled fabric rosette flowers in a variety of colors.

5 Using a handsewing needle and thread or fabric glue, attach rolled fabric rosette flowers along the top of the pillow and at the top of the stems.

6 Continue to build up the surface with rosettes, alternating colors and sizes.

7 With wrong sides together, sew the front pillow and the remaining painted fabric pillow back around all four sides with a closely spaced zigzag stitch, leaving an opening of about 3" (7.5 cm) on one side.

8 Fill the pillow with polyester stuffing, inserting it through the opening a little at a time. When the pillow is as firm as you like, close the opening with handstitching.

To make rolled rosette flowers:

note: *See the DVD included with this book for a demonstration of this technique.*

1 Start with a strip of fabric measuring about 1" x 12" (2.5 x 30.5 cm). Tie a knot at one of end of the strip and begin twisting and rolling the strip around the knot, dabbing fabric glue as you roll (or using a hot glue gun).

2 Continue rolling and twisting the strip until you reach the end.

3 Secure the end of the fabric by gluing it to the back of the flower.

4 Repeat to make additional rosettes, using longer strips to make larger flowers.

Rosette Pillow back

GRaFFITI
ZIPPER BAG

A LITTLE ZIPPERED BAG FULL OF COLOR, texture, and graffiti words is the perfect accessory for jeans or a cocktail dress. Make this bag for cosmetics or necessities for a night on the town. Begin by building a background for lettering and then add a zipper the easy way, with simple zigzag stitching.

FINISHED SIZE

7⅜" x 9" (19 x 23 cm)

MATERIALS

8" x 20" (20.5 x 51 cm) thin batting or fleece

8" x 20" (20.5 x 51 cm) fabric for bag lining

Scraps of painted, stamped, and altered fabric, enough to cover the surface of the batting or fleece and to make Two to three graffiti-style words and shapes

12" (30.5 cm) polyester zipper

Thread in desired colors

TOOLS

Fabric scissors

Permanent marker to outline words on fabric

Sewing machine with zipper foot

1   Select a variety of fabric scraps in different shapes, with an eye for color and texture.

2   Cut the batting or fleece into two pieces, each 8" x 10" (20.5 x 25.5 cm). Arrange fabric scraps on each batting surface. Experiment with creating a pattern, alternating colors and creating a surface full of visual interest. When you're satisfied with your arrangement, pin the fabric scraps in place.

3   Sew the scraps in place with messy stitching along the sides and corners of the scraps. Add a layer of messy stitching and stitched "scribbles" to the surface.

4   With the permanent marker, draw graffiti-style letters and words on brightly colored scraps. Cut the letters out. Arrange and pin the letters to the stitched surfaces, overlapping the letters.

5   Using a closely spaced zigzag stitch and contrasting thread, sew along the outlines of the letters until the entire word has stitching around it.

6   Cut your lining fabric into two pieces, each 8" x 10" (20.5 x 25.5 cm). Pin a piece of lining fabric to each stitched piece, wrong sides together, and attach lining and bag pieces with more messy stitches.

7   Place one side of the quilted fabric right side up and place the zipper underneath. Place the top of the zipper tape about ¼" (6 mm) from one edge; the zipper will extend beyond the other edge. Place the top edge of the bag along the zipper tape at least

⅛" (3 mm) from zipper teeth. Pin in place. Using the zipper foot, stitch with a very closely spaced zigzag stitch along the edge of the quilted fabric, removing the pins as you go **(fig. 1)**.

8   Pin and sew the other side of the quilted bag to the other side of the zipper, making sure that the zipper is centered **(fig. 2)**.

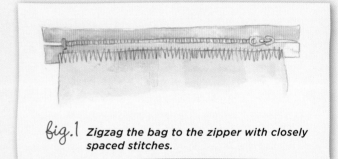

fig.1 **Zigzag the bag to the zipper with closely spaced stitches.**

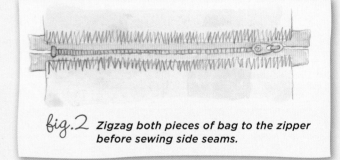

fig.2 **Zigzag both pieces of bag to the zipper before sewing side seams.**

9 To stitch the sides and the bottom of the bag together, fold the bag right sides together and sew the sides of the bag in a ¼" (6 mm) seam with straight stitch. On the end where the zipper teeth extend beyond the bag, you should be able to carefully stitch right through the zipper teeth as long as you're using a polyester zipper.

10 Unzip the zipper.

11 Sew the bottom of the bag in a ¼" (6 mm) seam with straight stitch.

12 Using zigzag stitch, go over the side and bottom seams, sewing both seam allowances together.

13 Turn bag right side out.

ROMANTiC RUFFLe
APRON

A CREATIVE AND MESSY GAL always needs to have a fun apron on hand. Colorful handmade fabrics in different patterns are perfect for stacking ruffles and creating a fun, flirty ruffled apron. I handpainted each fabric strip in one or two colors with different motifs on each one. Wear this apron in the kitchen, in the studio, or just around the house.

FINISHED SIZE

17" x 17" (43 x 43 cm) apron
with 20" (51 cm) ties

MATERIALS

18" x 18" (45.5 x 45.5 cm) piece of plain woven fabric for the foundation panel of the apron

Six strips of painted, printed, and altered fabric for ruffles, each 4" X 24" (10 x 61 cm) or ruffles as shown or 4" x 36" (10 x 91.5 cm) for fuller ruffles

5" X 58" (12.5 x 147.5 cm) strip of painted or printed fabric for waistband and ties

Thread in desired colors

TOOLS

Fabric scissors

Pins

Sewing machine

1 Hem the bottom and sides of the 18″ × 18″ (45.5 × 45.5 cm) panel by folding under ¼″ (6 mm) of the fabric and then folding over again. Press and machine stitch.

2 Hem the sides and the bottom of each of the six ruffle fabric strips in the same fashion.

3 Using a long straight machine stitch, stitch along the top of the unhemmed edge of each of the fabric strips, about ½″ (1.3 cm) from the edge. Do not backstitch. (**NOTE:** If making fuller ruffles, add a second row of long straight stitches about ¼″ [6 mm] from the edge of the fabric.)

4 Pull the bobbin thread or threads along the unhemmed edge of each ruffle to gather it to about 18″ (45.5 cm) long **(fig. 1)**.

5 Lay the foundation panel right side up. Pin the top edge of one ruffle to the fabric, adjusting it so the bottom edge of the ruffle extends slightly below the bottom of the foundation panel, and adjusting gathers so that the sides of the ruffle meet the edges of the foundation panel **(fig. 2)**.

6 Stitch the ruffle to the foundation panel along the top edge of the ruffle.

7 Pin and sew the next ruffle to the foundation panel, making sure that the ruffle overlaps the top edge of the ruffle below it.

fig.1   **Pull bobbin threads to gather ruffle.**

fig.2   **Pin first ruffle to cover bottom hemmed edge of apron panel.**

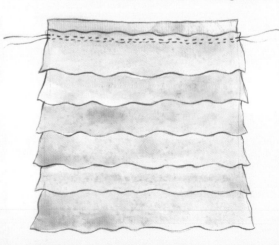

fig.3   **Each ruffle should slightly overlap the ruffle below, covering stitching.**

8   Repeat with the remaining ruffles. The top ruffle should fall about 1″ (2.5 cm) below the top edge of the foundation panel **(fig. 3)**.

9   To make the waistband and ties, fold the 5″ × 58″ (12.5 × 147.5 cm) piece of fabric in half lengthwise, wrong sides together.

10 Stitch around all the raw edges of the folded strip with a closely spaced zigzag stitch.

11 Pin the strip to the top of the apron on the right side, matching the top edges of the ruffle and apron, and matching the center of the apron and the center of the waistband so that there is equal length remaining for the ties on each side.

12 Sew the waistband/tie strip across its width with several rows of stitches.

improvisationaL
ART QUILTS

I JUST DON'T HAVE THE PATIENCE, discipline, or focus to tackle a traditional quilt. Instead, I love putting my own twist on the basic concept of quilting—the process of stitching two layers of fabric together with a layer of batting in between. My take on quilts, big or small, is all about expression—my quilts are freeform, messy, and full of texture. They have the look and feel of an art quilt. Use any of the surface design techniques in this book to create fabric for your scraps, backing, and binding.

FINISHED SIZES

This quilt can be made in any size. As shown:

Small quilt: 11¾" x 15" (30 x 38 cm)

Medium quilt: 32½" x 33½" (82.5 x 85 cm)

Large quilt: 43½" x 56" (110.5 x 142 cm)

MATERIALS

Painted and altered fabric scraps in a variety of shapes and sizes (enough to cover the surface of your quilt)

Fusible lightweight interfacing to match size of quilt (cut pieces of interfacing to fit if necessary)

Two pieces of thin batting, each the size of your quilt

Fabric for backing in the size of your quilt

Strips of fabric for binding, enough for all four sides of the quilt (for smaller quilts, strips should be about 2½" [5.5 cm] wide; for larger quilts, 4" [10 cm] wide)

Thread in at least two colors

TOOLS

Fabric scissors

Press cloth (generous scrap of muslin or other plain woven fabric)

Iron

Sewing machine

Small quilt

1. Start by selecting a variety of fabric scraps in different shapes and sizes, choosing colors and textures that work together.

2. With the adhesive side of the fusible interfacing facing up, arrange fabric scraps on the surface of the interfacing (if necessary, align pieces of interfacing to create a surface that is the size of the desired finished quilt). Experiment with creating a pattern with the fabric scraps by alternating colors and creating a surface full of visual interest.

3. Once the entire surface is filled with scraps in a pleasing arrangement, place a press cloth over the fabric scraps and press with a warm iron to lightly fuse the scraps to the interfacing and hold them in place.

4. Place the interfacing with fused fabric scraps (the quilt top) on top of your batting and pin down.

5. Begin to machine stitch the quilt top to the batting. Use different kinds of stitching inside of the different fabric sections, use lots of messy stitches along the sides and corners of the scraps, drop the feed dog and add a layer of free-motion stitching to the surface—as with all of the stitching projects here, be playful and enjoy the process.

6. Spread out the backing fabric, wrong side up. Lay your second piece of batting on top of the backing. Finally, put your stitched quilt top on top of the bat-

ting. This is your "quilt sandwich." Pin together.

7 Thread your machine with another color of thread and quilt all the layers together with a repetitive stitch (straight, doodles, circles, etc.). This is the stitching that will show on the back of the quilt.

8 With scissors or rotary cutter, neaten the edges of the quilt if needed.

9 Fold a binding strip over one edge so that there is slightly more fabric on the wrong side than on the front. Press and pin in place. Follow with a binding strip on the next edge (overlapping the first strip at the corner), until you have binding strips pinned around the entire quilt. There's no need to turn in the side edges of the binding; I leave the edges unfinished and allow them to fray.

10 Sew the binding strips down with zigzag stitches, messy straight stitches, or even machine doodles to add another stitched element on the binding.

Medium quilt

fAbuLous FusioN
TOTE BAG

A TOTE BAG JUST MIGHT BE ONE OF the most versatile items to have on hand—it's functional for trips to the grocery store and it's also a great way to express yourself and carry a little unique art on your arm. This pretty tote is virtuous, too— it incorporates fused plastic bags, recycled fabric from old clothing, and painted fabric.

FINISHED SIZE

12" x 13½" (30.5 x 34.5 cm) plus straps

* *Target Corporation is not a sponsor of this project and is not affiliated with Sew Wild, Alisa Burke, or Interweave.*

MATERIALS

Four to six plastic bags (I used Target* bags)

Squares of painted fabric and recycled fabric in various sizes

26" x 14" (66 x 35.5 cm) interfacing or thin batting

26" x 14" (66 x 35.5 cm) fabric for lining

1" x 44" (2.5 x 112 cm) canvas webbing for handles

Thread in desired colors

TOOLS

Iron

Press cloth

Pins

Sewing machine

Pencil or fabric marking pen

1 Using the iron and press cloth, and following the instructions on page 68, fuse the plastic bags. Cut the fused plastic into squares of various sizes.

2 Cut the interfacing, fleece, or batting into two pieces, each 13" x 14" (33 x 35.5 cm). These will be the two sides of the tote. Arrange your squares of painted and recycled fabric and fused plastic on the surface of the interfacing, fleece, or batting in a pleasing design. Pin the squares down and trim any edges that extend beyond the foundation.

3 Using a zigzag stitch, sew all of the squares to the surface of the interfacing. Fill both pieces of interfacing completely with sewn-down squares.

4 Cut the lining fabric into two pieces, each 13" x 14" (33 x 35.5 cm). Place a piece of lining fabric wrong side up and place the interfacing with stitched squares right side up on top of the lining fabric.

5 Using a straight stitch, quilt the two layers together by stitching back and forth across the entire surface. Don't worry about making the stitching perfect; you can even use messy stitches, curved stitches, or creative stitching. Repeat for the second piece of lining and interfacing with stitched squares.

6 Using a closely spaced zigzag stitch, stitch across one 13" (33 cm) edge of each piece; these will be the top edges of the panels.

7 On each panel, at the top edge, use a pencil or fabric marking pen to mark 3" (7.5 cm) from each end.

8 Cut the canvas strap in half to make two handles. Pin the handles to the lining side of each panel at the markings made in Step 7, with the bottom edges of the straps about 1" (2.5 cm) below the top edge of the panels. Sew straps down. Place the panels right sides together, top edges matching, and sew the sides and bottom in a ¼" (6 mm) seam.

9 While the tote is still wrong sides out, fold each corner into a triangle and sew down with a straight stitch about 2" (5 cm) from corner to form the base of the bag **(fig. 1)**.

10 Turn the bag right side out.

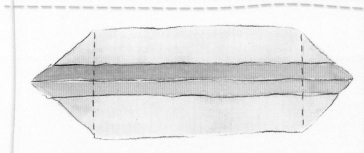

fig.1 **Fold corners at bottom of bag and stitch.**

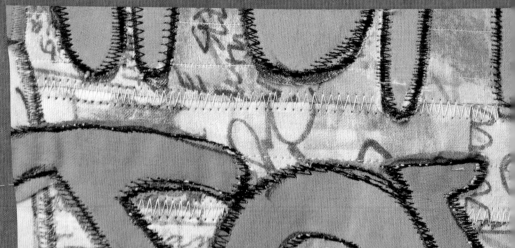

GRaFFITI
PILLOW

INSPIRED BY THE BOLD LETTERING IN GRAFFITI, this pillow makes use of fabric that is full of text, lettering, and layers of messy color, with big lettering layered and sewn to the top. Keep contrast in mind when designing your pillow and pick vibrant colors that will make the words pop.

FINISHED SIZE

14" x 14" (35.5 x 35.5 cm)

MATERIALS

32" x 16" (81.5 x 40.5 cm) interfacing or batting

16" x 16" (40.5 x 40.5 cm) fabric for pillow back

Four to five strips of plain fabric suitable for painting, each 3" to 4" x 17" (7.5 to 10 x 43 cm), and one strip about 7" x 13" (18 x 33 cm)

Paints and markers to decorate fabric

12 to 14 oz (340 to 397 g) polyester fiberfill stuffing

Thread in desired colors

TOOLS

Fabric scissors

Pins

Sewing machine

Handsewing needle

1   Cut the interfacing or batting into two 16″ x 16″ (40.5 x 40.5 cm) pieces.

2   Paint and alter the strips of plain fabric with paint, text, and words, covering the surface of each. Paint a large graffiti-style word on the 7″ x 13″ (18 x 33 cm) fabric.

3   Using the strips of fabric covered in text, cover one piece of interfacing or batting. Pin the strips in place and sew to the interfacing with messy stitching.

4   Cut out the large graffiti-style word and pin onto the layered surface. I have centered the word "LOVE," but you could have fun experimenting with placement.

5   Using a closely spaced zigzag stitch, sew along the outside of the letters until the entire word has stitching around it.

6   Place the square of backing fabric on top of the second piece of interfacing. Sew straight-stitch lines or messy stitches until you have stitching no less than 2″ to 3″ (5 to 7.5 cm) apart all over.

7   Place the pillow front and pillow back with right sides together. Pin around all four sides.

8   Sew all sides together with a straight stitch in a ½″ (1.3 cm) seam, leaving an opening of about 3″ (7.5 cm) on one side.

9   Turn pillow right side out through opening and fill with polyester stuffing. Close the opening with handstitching.

FLOWER GARDEN
FABRIC WREATH

THIS UNIQUE FIBER WREATH is perfect for holidays or
to celebrate any change of season; just change the colors and
decorations to suit the time of year. Give it as a gift or use it as
a home accent. This wreath makes use of all those tiny scraps
of fabric and odd material that you don't know what to do with,
transforming them into a beautiful accent for a door or hallway.

FINISHED SIZE

Wreath base is 15¾"
(40 cm) in diameter

MATERIALS

Styrofoam wreath form

2" x 48" (5 x 122 cm) strip of fabric to wrap
wreath base

Scraps of fabric and paper (I used old book
pages and recycled papers)

Acrylic paint and dye to decorate fabric and paper

Thread in desired colors

TOOLS

Hot glue gun

Fabric scissors

Paper scissors

Paintbrush

Sewing machine

3   With the sewing machine, using free-motion and zigzag stitching, "draw" details on the leaves.

4   Create flowers for the wreath using free-motion machine stitching to doodle and draw simple flowers on fabric. Add small center circles from scraps of fabric for color, contrast, and variation.

5   Cut around the flower doodles in circular shapes and zigzag-stitch around the shape for added definition.

6   Cover the top of the wreath with a layer of leaves by applying hot glue to the middle of each leaf and attaching to the wreath. Alternate leaves with different colors and patterns until the surface of the wreath is covered.

7   Add another layer of leaves with the hot glue gun to cover as much of the wreath surface as possible and to create the look and feel of layers.

8   Add the flowers to the top of the leaves. Position them evenly around the surface of the wreath and secure with hot glue gun.

1   Start by wrapping the wreath form with the long strip of fabric. Using hot glue, secure one end of the fabric strip to the wreath, wrap around and secure with more glue as you wrap. Continue to wrap strip around the wreath until the entire wreath is covered, as shown in photograph at right.

2   Create leaves from scraps of paper and fabric by cutting out simple leaf shapes, painting them, and layering them on top of each other. Use paper or craft scissors for paper and fabric scissors for fabric.

Flower Garden Fabric Wreath, underside.

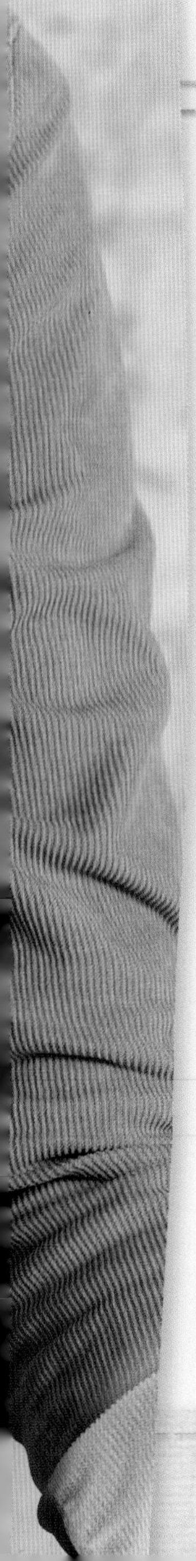

cozy jersey
SCARF

RECYCLING FABRIC IS SUCH A GREAT WAY to breath new life into the things that you already have on hand. We all have old t-shirts, and the jersey knit fabric is the perfect material for dyeing, painting, and transforming with various techniques. Jersey is soft and flexible, perfect for a colorful and creative scarf. You can adapt this method to just about any fabric that you have on hand, such as linen, cotton, or fleece.

FINISHED SIZE

4" x 70" (10 x 178 cm)

MATERIALS

9" x 70" (23 x 178 cm) solid color jersey knit fabric

Painted and altered t-shirt and jersey fabric scraps in a variety of colors

Thread in desired colors

TOOLS

Fabric scissors

Pins

Sewing machine

Sewing machine needle for knit fabrics

1   Using the colorful painted and altered t-shirt scraps, cut out a variety of strips, squares, and shapes.

2   Arrange the scraps on the 9" x 70" (23 x 178 cm) strip of jersey. Experiment with layering scraps on top of each other and stacking contrasting colors, sizes, and shapes. When you're satisfied with the design, pin the scraps to the foundation strip.

3   Using a sewing machine with a needle made for knits, sew the scraps to the foundation strip. Use messy stitching around shapes and corners and free-motion stitching to create details and additional lines.

4   When all the scraps are attached and you're satisfied with the stitching, fold the scarf in half along the long dimension with right sides together.

5   Using a narrow zigzag stitch, sew the long side of the scarf in a ½" (1.3 cm) seam. Leave the short sides open for turning.

6   Turn the scarf right side out. Using messy zigzag stitching, sew the ends of the scarf together.

SWEET AND MESSY
BUCKET HAT

THIS WHIMSICAL BUCKET HAT, sized for an adult or a child, utilizes handmade fabric and messy stitching. The concept is easy and the design is simple. But your creativity turns this hat into a fabulous fashion accessory. I demonstrate the method for making this simple fabric flower in the DVD that's included with this book.

FINISHED SIZES

Pattern templates are included for small (child), medium, and large (adult) sizes.

Small: Crown diameter 5½" (14 cm); band circumference 20½" (52 cm)

Medium: Crown diameter 6¼" (16 cm); band circumference 22" (56 cm)

Large: Crown diameter 6⅝" (17 cm); band circumference 23½" (59.5 cm)

MATERIALS

For hat:
½ yd (45.5 cm) of lightweight interfacing (use fleece for a softer hat)
Painted fabric scraps (½ yd [45.5 cm] total)
½ yd (45.5 cm) of 45" (114.5 cm) wide fabric for lining
Thread in desired colors

For fabric flower:
Painted or printed fabric scraps, 3" to 4" (7.5 to 10 cm) wide (or in diameter, if circular)

TOOLS

For hat:
Pattern templates Band A, Brim B, Crown C* (pages 138–139)
Fabric scissors
Pins
Sewing machine
Hot glue gun, fabric glue, or handsewing needle
Enlarge pattern pieces on a copy machine as directed on template.

For fabric flower:
Fabric scissors
Hot glue gun

To make hat:

1 Enlarge, trace, and cut out pattern templates A, B, and C in the correct size from interfacing. Transfer notches and mark centers.

2 Arrange and pin fabric scraps and pieces to the surface of the three interfacing pieces.

3 Using messy free-motion stitching, sew the scraps onto the surface of all pattern pieces. Trim scraps to fit interfacing as needed.

4 Trace and cut out pattern templates A, B, and C from lining fabric. Pin the corresponding lining piece to each hat piece, wrong sides together.

5 Use messy stitching to attach the lining and hat pieces.

6 Finish the raw edge of the brim with a closely spaced zigzag stitch.

7 Right sides together, pin notched edge of Band A to notched edge of Brim B. Ease as necessary to fit. Stitch in a ¼" (6 mm) seam with straight stitch **(fig.1)**.

8 Stitch seam allowances together with closely spaced zigzag stitch.

9 Right sides together, stitch side seam of band/brim in a ¼" (6 mm) seam with straight stitch. Stitch seam allowances together with closely spaced zigzag stitch.

10 Right sides together, pin the top edge of the band to the crown, matching center fronts and matching crown center back to band side seam. Use plenty of pins **(fig. 2)**. Stitch in a ¼" (6 mm) seam with straight stitch. Stitch seam allowances together with closely spaced zigzag stitch.

11 Turn hat right side out. Make fabric flower as instructed below and attach fabric flower with glue gun, fabric glue, or a few handstitches.

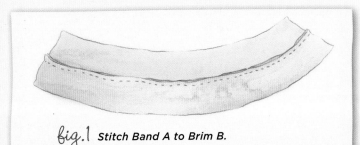

fig.1 **Stitch Band A to Brim B.**

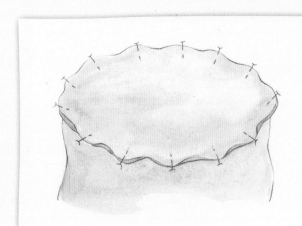

fig.2 **Pin crown of hat to band, easing to fit.**

To make fabric flower:

note: *See the DVD included with this book for a demonstration of this technique.*

1 Cut a circle from painted or printed fabric in the size desired; mine are 3″ to 4″ (7.5 to 10 cm) in diameter.

2 Fold another circular scrap of fabric into quarters. Using a hot glue gun, glue the center of the wrong side of the folded scrap to the center of the right side of the circle.

3 Fold another scrap, of any shape, into quarters and repeat Step 2, gluing it very close to the first scrap.

4 Continue adding folded scraps to the base circle with the hot glue gun, placing them very close together.

5 When the circle is filled with folded scraps, trim any edges that are sticking out to create a dome shape. Your flower is complete!

schematic

Bucket Hat, front view

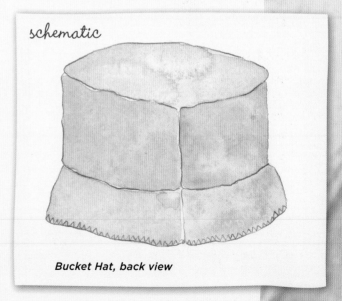

schematic

Bucket Hat, back view

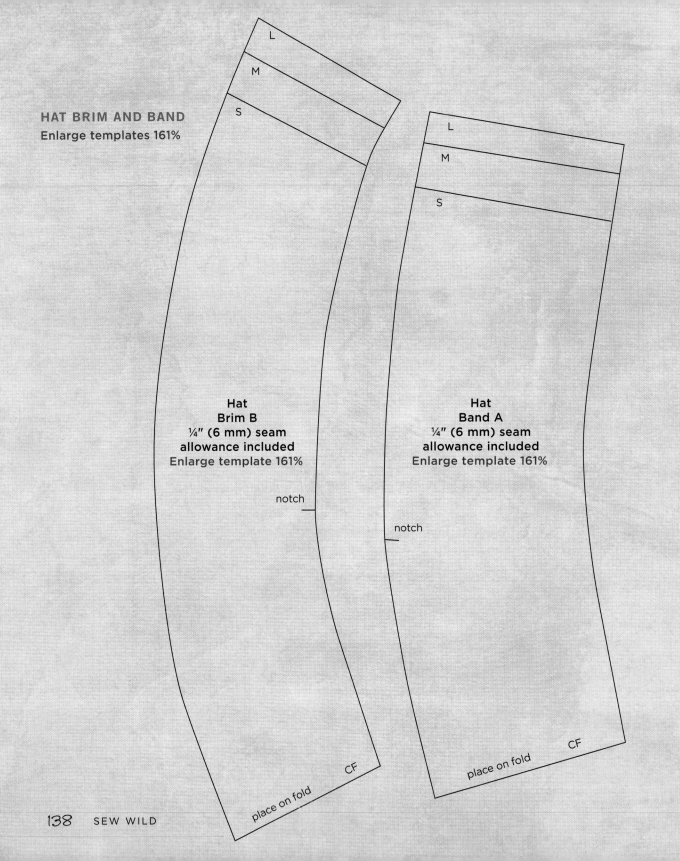

HAT BRIM AND BAND
Enlarge templates 161%

L

M

S

**Hat
Brim B**
¼" (6 mm) seam
allowance included
Enlarge template 161%

notch

L

M

S

**Hat
Band A**
¼" (6 mm) seam
allowance included
Enlarge template 161%

notch

place on fold   CF

place on fold   CF

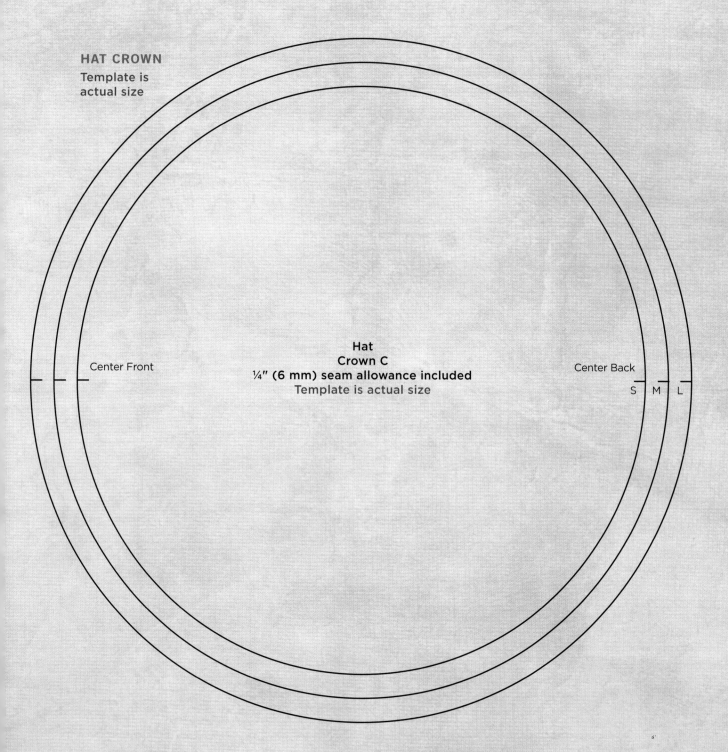

HAT CROWN
Template is
actual size

Center Front

**Hat
Crown C
¼″ (6 mm) seam allowance included**
Template is actual size

Center Back

S M L

Conclusion

NOW THAT YOU HAVE THE TOOLS AND THE INSPIRATION, it's time to put them to use! Forget about the rules and give yourself permission to play. Try using the surface design techniques I've shared or come up with your own. Experiment with color, texture, and layers, and create unique fabric that represents your style. Rip, cut, and redefine your fabric and use it in sewing projects. Explore the sewing machine with a sense of freedom. Use your stitching as a form of expression or as another element in your surface design. It's time to break rules, find your style, to let loose, and sew wild!

RECOMMENDED READING

Arnett, William, et al. *The Quilts of Gee's Bend: Master-pieces from a Lost Place.* Atlanta, Georgia: Tinwood Books, 2002.

Bennett, Cat. *The Confident Creative: Drawing to Free the Hand and Mind.* Forres, Scotland: Findhorn Press, 2010.

Dorit, Elisha. *Printmaking + Mixed Media: Simple Tech-niques and Projects for Paper and Fabric.* Loveland, Colorado: Interweave, 2009.

Finlay, Victoria. *Color: A Natural History of the Palette.* New York: Random House, 2003.

Gillow, John. *Indian Textiles.* London: Thames & Hudson, 2008.

Kinard, Lyric. *Art + Quilt: Design Principles and Creativity Exercises.* Loveland, Colorado: Interweave, 2009.

Meller, Susan, and Susan Elffers. *Textile Designs: Two Hundred Years of European and American Patterns Or-ganized by Motif, Style, Color, Layout, and Period.* New York: Harry N. Abrams, 2002.

Parramon, Jose. *Color Theory* (Watson-Guptill Artist's Library). New York: Watson-Guptill, 1989.

Testa, Melanie. *Inspired to Quilt: Creative Experiments in Art Quilt Imagery.* Loveland, Colorado: Interweave, 2009.

Salamony, Sandra. *1,000 Artisan Textiles: Contemporary Fiber Art, Quilts, and Wearables.* Beverly, Massachu-setts: Quarry Books, 2010.

Sonheim, Carla. *Drawing Lab for Mixed-Media Artists: 52 Creative Exercises to Make Drawing Fun.* Beverly, Massachusetts: Quarry Books, 2010.

RESOURCES

Bernina of America

Berninausa.com

*Bernina sewing machines
(I use a Bernina Aurora 430)*

iLoveToCreate

ilovetocreate.com

One-step dye, fabric markers, fabric paint

Plaid

plaidonline.com

Paint, screenprinting ink, and other craft supplies

Ranger Ink

rangerink.com

Distributors of Claudine Hellmuth Studio mixed-media products

Rit Dye

ritdye.com

Easy-to-use all-purpose fabric dye made for home use

Rupert, Gibbon + Spider

jacquardproducts.com

Dye-Na-Flow liquid color for fabric and other textile paints and dyes

Sharpie

sharpie.com

Permanent markers in many colors and tip styles

Speedball Art Products

speedballart.com

Printmaking supplies, including inks, carving tools, and carving blocks

INDEX

Stitch up a storm